Handbook of JARGONS for Banking and Investments

An Essential Handbook for Finance Professionals

THOLOOR MATHEW THOMAS

notionpress.com

INDIA • SINGAPORE • MALAYSIA

ISBN 979-8-89277-893-0

Contents

Preface

The world of Banking and Investments is filled with acronyms and industry specific terms which can sometimes be difficult to find easily. This book is intended to bring to you most of the jargons currently used in banking, investments, finance and economics. As more and more terms are being added to the financial world on a consistent basis, this book doesn't claim to be an all en-compassing guide, but will serve as a reference book for most of the important terms prevailing as of the time of publishing this book. This book is designed for a wider audience. Hence this book will be a ready reference for those appearing for competitive examinations in banking, finance and investments and for bankers, investment analysts, investment professionals, investors, currency traders, and for students of finance.

This book is the combined product of my qualifications, more than forty years of my experience in banking, investments, foreign exchange, and international capital markets. The hands - on experience, I gained in banking, investments, including money market products, bonds, equities and alternative investments and treasury operations, has been a special asset in producing this book. This book is my attempt to find a common ground between theory, applications and examples, and to provide a guide for those who not only want to practice but also want to enhance their knowledge in the financial world.

This handbook starts with an introduction to financial investments and then discusses the key terms relating to various investment assets, banking, foreign exchange, corporate finance, and economics. I believe the primary strength of this book is its focus on international markets, without underweighting relevant terms relating to the Indian financial environment. I have also tried to incorporate in this book all branches of the capital markets.

Each chapter begins with an opener which provides a brief introduction to the subject covered in the chapter to provide the readers a quick understanding of the contents in the chapter. This book has been written to make investment literature easier to understand and to clarify some of the most commonly used terms in India and abroad. Emphasis has been placed on clarity rather than attempting to cover every single complex detail.

It is my hope that this book will serve as a good resource for learners as well as practitioners in the world of banking and investments due to its coverage of investment assets in the global marketplace. I hope you will find this book useful and simple to digest. I have made every effort to ensure that the terms are accurately described, however, the descriptions are not definitive and they may differ from the interpretations used in other contexts.

Thank you for choosing this handbook. I wish you a pleasant reading.

About the Author

Tholoor M. Thomas is a retired Investment professional and a banker with over 40 years of experience in investment management and banking. He is a Chartered Financial Analyst (CFA) from the CFA Institute, USA, a holder of LLB (Gen) from Mumbai University, a B.Sc from University of Kerala, a holder of certificate from Indian Institute of Bankers, Mumbai and a holder of certificate from New York Institute of Finance.

Mr. Thomas is a seasoned investment manager. He retired as Director of Investments from a leading reinsurance group in the Kingdom of Bahrain after serving the company for more than 29 years in various roles in its investment function. He also served in the Finance and Treasury function of a leading industrial company in the Kingdom of Bahrain for 6 years. Prior to that he was employed in the Foreign Exchange department of State Bank of India, Mumbai for 6 years. As an investment manager, he has managed an international multi-asset investment portfolio of significant size with assets in Short-term investments, Bonds, Equities, Alternative Investments comprising private equity, venture capital, real estate, mortgage-backed securities, and hedge funds. In his role as Director of Investments, he was responsible for managing an investment department employing about 15 investment professionals. As part of his investment career, he had hands-on experience in major global stock markets from Tokyo stock exchange to Wall Street. In addition, he has managed a multi-currency bond portfolio of substantial size for his employer.

Mr. Thomas has previously written two books – "The Bull Run" and "Inside the Foreign Exchange Universe." He has also written several articles on investments and financial subjects for key magazines and publications. He has delivered several speeches in investment forums and investment professional chapters. Thomas has won several financial forecast competitions held by leading global financial institutions, including the Treasury financial forecast of exchange rates held among the investment managers of the entire GCC region by Citicorp. He has rendered a commendable service to the CFA society in Bahrain by discharging the role of Chief Proctor for the CFA examinations held in Bahrain and by holding several positions in the CFA society there. Mr. Thomas was highly regarded among the investment community in the GCC region for his analytical and investment decision making skills. He is credited as the first user of the Bloomberg financial and information system in the whole of Middle East. He is also known as the first investment manager from Middle East to invest in mortgage-backed securities when such securities were issued for the first time outside the US market.

Having started his investment and banking career in the '70s, Mr. Thomas has seen the growth of global capital markets from Tokyo Stock Exchange to New York Stock Exchange. He has also seen how the global Forex market developed from a primitive stage to what it is now. In terms of global Fixed Income market, he has seen the explosion in the volume of international debt market. In the complicated Alternative Investment space, Mr. Thomas was an active participant in many of the assets which were introduced in the Alternative asset class.

CHAPTER 1

Financial Investments – A Short Introduction

Financial Investments

Investment is the commitment of money to purchase an asset to attain an increase in value over a period of time. Investment involves the sacrifice of some assets now, such as money, time, and effort for a future gain. A financial investment is the investment in a financial product with the aim of making money. Investment has some risks specific to the asset that you invest in. Such risks weigh on your decision to invest and determine the time, amount, and the mode of your investment. Investing is an effective way to put your money to work and build wealth over a period of time. But those who take the time to understand the basic principles of investing stand to benefit significantly over the long haul.

Types of Financial Assets

There is a range of financial assets available for investing. A financial asset's worth is based on its risk, supply, demand, liquidity, and various other factors. Hence such factors influence the investment appetite for a financial asset. Based on the relative riskiness of various asset classes, key financial assets are ranked from lowest risk to highest risk as follows:

- Cash & Money market investments (such as CDs, Treasury Bills)
- Government Bonds & Corporate Bonds
- Equities, including equity mutual funds, ETFs, and Index based securities
- Futures and Options
- Real Estate
- Commodities
- Currencies (Foreign Exchange)
- Alternative Investments, such as Private equity, Hedge funds, and Venture Capital
- Cryptocurrency

Investment Risks

All financial investments are subject to various types of risks. Some of the important risks are:

- Market risk (Risk of decline in value due to various factors such as economic factors, interest rate changes, currency fluctuations and equity price changes)
- Liquidity risk (Risk of being unable to sell an investment at a fair price when required)
- Credit risk (Risk that a bond issuer such as a government or corporate entity is unable to pay interest and principal repayment)
- Inflation Risk (Inflation erodes the purchasing power of money)
- Political Risk (Political events, war, civil disturbances etc.)

Investment Return

The various types of return on financial investments are:

- Interest
- Dividends
- Capital gain
- Currency Gain

Investment Policy

An investor should have an investment policy stating the investment objectives, constraints, asset allocation parameters, type of investment assets, investment horizon, risk tolerance and various other factors.

Investment Management

Investment management is the professional asset management of financial assets. It helps people protect their hard-earned money and helps grow money over a certain period of time.

Types of Investors

The type of investors in financial investments consists of:

- Personal Investors
- Angel Investors
- Venture Capitalists
- Incubators
- Banks and Financial Institutions
- Corporate Investors
- Sovereign Wealth Funds
- Supranational Entities

CHAPTER 2

Money Market

Money Market

The Money Market is an organized exchange marketplace, wherein, the participants can either borrow or lend money through short-term debt instruments having an average maturity of one year or less. The debt instruments may be traded at wholesale and retail levels. At wholesale level, it involves large size trades between traders and institutions. At retail level, it involves money market mutual funds purchased by individual investors and bank customers. Money market instruments in India comprise: (1) call money, (2) certificates of deposit, (3) treasury bills, (4) other short-term securities such as REPOs, (5) bankers' acceptances/ commercial bills, (6) commercial paper and (7) inter-corporate funds. Investment risk in money market instruments is comparatively lower due to the short-term maturity period. The common terms used in the Money market are described below:

1. Accretion of a Discount

Accretion is an accounting process by which the book value of a security purchased at a discount from par is increased during the holding period of that security. In other words accretion is the increase in the security's value as it nears maturity. At maturity the book value equals par. For example, if a security with a face value of

Rs.100 and a remaining maturity of 100 days is purchased at Rs.99, the daily accretion on a straight-line basis is one paisa. Hence the book value of the security will increase by one paisa each day,from Rs.99 at the purchase time to Rs.100 at the security's maturity. The Treasury bills issued by RBI are issued at a discount and redeemed at maturity at their face value.

2. Amortization of a premium

Amortization is an accounting process by which the book value of a security purchased at a premium above par is decreased during the holding period of that security. In other words, amortization is the decrease in the security's value as it nears maturity. At maturity the book value equals par. For example, if a security with a face value of Rs.100 and a remaining maturity of 100 days is purchased at Rs.101, the daily amortization on a straight-line basis is one paisa. Hence the book value of the security will decrease by one paisa per day from Rs.101 at the purchase time to Rs.100 at the security's maturity.

3. Annualized Yield

A rate of return for a given period that is less or more than one year, but that is adjusted to show the return that would equate to over a one year period. In other words it is the geometric average amount of money earned by an investment each year over a given time period.

4. Ask price

The price at which a market maker will sell a security

5. Basis point (bp)

One bp is one-hundredth of 1 percent (0.01 percent). 100 basis points equal 1 percent.

6. Central Bank Bills

Short-term securities issued by a Central Bank which is marketable or tradable.

7. Certificate of Deposit (CD)

A savings certificate, generally issued by a commercial bank, that entitles the bearer to receive interest.

8. Commercial Paper (CP)

Short-term, unsecured notes issued by a corporation to meet short-term cash requirement.

9. Credit rating

An evaluation of a security's creditworthiness given by a rating agency.

10. Credit risk

The risk of default by an issuer of a debt security.

11. Credit spread

The incremental yield required for a debt security above that of a risk-free alternative. For example, the yield on a commercial paper compared to a similar maturity Government security's yield.

12. Default

The failure by a debt issuer to pay interest when due and pay principal on maturity of the debt.

13. Discount security

Non-interest bearing money market instrument that is issued at a discount to the maturity value.

14. Eurodollar Deposit

U.S. Dollar denominated deposit at foreign banks or foreign branches of U.S. banks.

15. Federal Funds

Non - interest bearing deposits held at U.S Federal Reserve by member banks.

16. Interest rate risk

The risk of gain or loss on the value of a security due to changes in interest rates.

17. Liquidity

The ability of a security to be easily converted to cash without substantial loss.

18. LIBOR

London Interbank Rate (LIBOR) is the interest rate at which banks offer to lend among themselves in the interbank market in London. It is calculated as an average of the indications received from banks in London. It is a key global benchmark for borrowing costs between banks.

19. Maturity Date

The final payment date of a debt security.

20. Primary Dealers

A bank or other financial institution that is approved to trade securities with a national government. Primary dealers buy government securities from the central bank and sell them to their clients, creating the initial market. As per RBI website some of the primary dealers include ICICI Securities Primary Dealership Limited, Morgan Stanley

India Primary Dealers Pvt. Ltd., Nomura Fixed Income Securities Pvt. Ltd., and SBI DFHI Ltd.

21. Repurchase Agreement (REPO)

A form of short-term funding for dealers.

22. Treasury Bill (T-bill)

A short-term debt obligation of the RBI with a maturity less than one year. It is issued to meet the short-term expenditure of the government or to regulate money supply in the economy. Various central banks issue T – bills of different maturities.

23. Yield

The annual rate of return from income paid out on an investment in debt securities.

24. Yield to Maturity (YTM)

The rate of return on a debt security held to maturity, considering the purchase price, interest payments and maturity value.

CHAPTER 3

Bonds

Bond (Fixed Income Security)

A Bond or a Fixed Income security is a loan from an investor to the issuer of the security. The issuer of the security pays a fixed pre-determined coupon to the investor at periodic intervals, as decided at the time of issue. The coupon may be at a fixed rate or a floating rate. There are also zero-coupon bonds and convertible bonds. Examples of Fixed Income securities are :

- Treasury Bills (T- Bills)
- Treasury Notes (T- Notes)
- Treasury Bonds (T-Bonds)
- Corporate Bonds
- Municipal Bonds ("munis")
- Certificates of Deposits (CDs)

Bond prices and interest rates are inversely correlated. When interest rates go up, bond prices fall and vice-versa. Most bonds are issued at par. The market price of a bond depends on a number of factors: the credit quality of the issuer, the length of time until maturity, and the coupon rate compared to prevailing interest rate environment. The face value of the bond is what the borrower pays to the investor on maturity of the bond.

In India there are mainly seven types of bonds an investor can invest in : 1) Government Bonds, 2) Corporate Bonds, 3) Convertible Bonds, 4) Zero Coupon Bonds, 5) Inflation Linked Bonds, 6) RBI Bonds and 7) Sovereign Gold Bonds.

1. Accrued interest

The interest receivable from a bond's last interest payment date up to the current date

2. Ask yield to maturity

The rate of return an investor receives if the bond is held to maturity date, calculated using the ask price

3. Basis point

One bp is one-hundredth of one percent (1/100 or 0.01)

4. Bid

The price at which a dealer is willing to purchase a bond

5. Bond convexity

The measure of the change in the bond duration for every 1% change in the market interest rates

6. Bond duration

Bond duration measures the percentage change in a bond's price with a 1% change in its yield level.

7. Bond option

Bond option is a contract between the buyer and seller to be executed in the future at a predefined time and price. There are basically two types of options – call option and put option. A call option gives the buyer the right but not the obligation to buy the bonds. A put option gives the seller a right but not an obligation to sell the bonds. Bonds with call option features are called callable bonds, and bonds with puttable options are called puttable bonds.

8. Bullet Bond

A security with a fixed maturity and no call feature

9. Callable bond

A bond which can be redeemed by the issuer before the scheduled maturity

10. Interest Rate Cap

The maximum interest rate that can be paid on a floating-rate security

11. Capital Gain Bonds (54EC Bonds)

54EC bonds are capital gain tax exemption bonds in India that provide 100% tax exemption on the long term capital gain earned by selling any property. The investment limit in 54EC bonds is Rs.50 lakhs. 54EC bonds do not provide any exemption on short term capital gains.

12. Carry

The cost of borrowing funds to finance a trading position

13. Collar

Upper and lower limits on the interest rate of a floating-rate security

14. Convertible bond

A feature in the bond which allows the investor to exchange the bond for a specified number of shares of common stock of the issuer

15. Conversion Price

The conversion price is the pre-set price at which the security can be converted into common stock. Usually, the conversion price is set at a price higher than the stock's price at the time of issue of the security.

16. Corporate Bond

A debt security issued by a corporation

17. Coupon

The interest rate a bond's issuer promises to pay to the bond holder until maturity or early redemption

18. Coupon frequency

The frequency with which a fixed-income security pays interest (e.g., quarterly, semi-annually, yearly)

19. Coupon rate

A bond's annual interest rate, expressed as a percentage of the bond's face value

20. Coupon type

How a bond's coupon is structured (e.g., Fixed, Variable, Zero, etc). Fixed coupon bonds give interest at a fixed rate (set at the issue time) to the lender on a periodic basis. Variable coupon bonds give interest at a rate determined periodically as per the terms of the bond. Zero coupon bond doesn't pay any interest, but trade at a deep discount. It is also known as accrual bond.

21. Credit Default Swap (CDS)

A credit default swap is a contract between two parties in which one party purchases a protection from the other party against losses from the default of a borrower within a defined period of time. CDS serves as an insurance against the default of the undelying borrower. To swap the risk of default, the lender buys a CDS from another investor who agrees to reimburse them if the borrower defaults

22. Credit quality

The credit criteria of a fixed-income security, expressed through the rating provided by a credit rating agency

23. Credit risk

The risk that the issuer of a fixed-income security may default on regular interest payments or principal payment at maturity

24. Creditor

An investor in bonds is termed as a creditor

25. Current yield

The ratio of the annual dollar amount of interest paid on a security to the purchase price or market price of the security, expressed as a percentage. For example, a Rs.1,000 bond purchased at par with a 5 percent coupon pays Rs.50 interest per year, which shows a current yield of 5%.

26. CUSIP

The nine-character alphanumeric identifier used to identify a U.S. or Canadian security. The acronym of CUSIP is **Committee on Uniform Security Identification Procedures.** In India the identifier is ISIN.

27. Day count convention

An indication of how many days in a month and days in a year are counted for interest calculations. Different markets use different

Day count basis for different securities. Some key day conventions are given below:

Description	Day count
Indian Government Securities*	30/360
Corporate bonds in India*	30 /360
U.S.Government Treasury bonds	Actual / 365
U.S Money market instruments	Actual / 360
London Interbank Offered Rate (LIBOR)	Actual / 360, except British Pound which uses Actual/ 365

*All months including February are considered as having 30days

28. Day order

An order to buy/sell a bond that is valid for the day

29. Debenture

A debenture is a debt instrument which is an insecure instrument. Debentures are secure only because of the creditworthiness of the issuer.

30. Default

A bond is said to be in default if the bond issuer fails to make periodic interest payment or payment of the principal amount at maturity.

31. Delivery

Delivery is the action by which a security trade is settled by receiving or delivering the security from/to the other party.

32. Delivery versus payment (DVP)

Delivery versus payment is a settlement method for securities market. It basically ensures the transfer of securities only after payment is made.

33. Discount

If a security is traded at a price below the 'face value' or par value, the security is at a discount. In a rising interest rate environment, existing bonds will tend to trade at a discount.

34. Domicile country

The country where the issuer of a security is incorporated

35. Duration

Duration is a measure of the sensitivity of the price of a bond to change in interest rates. Duration is stated in number of years.

36. Face value

The stated value of a debt security at maturity

37. FDIC

Federal Deposit Insurance Corporation

38. Federal funds rate

The interest rate charged by banks on overnight loans to other banks

39. Fill or kill order

This refers to the mode of execution of an order. This means that the order is to be executed in its entirety within a set time.

40. First coupon date

The date when the first interest payment from a newly issued bond will be made

41. First settlement date

The first settlement date of a newly issued bond, when a buyer must pay the seller for the securities delivered

42. Fixed Income Market

Fixed Income Market is a market for government bills and bonds and corporate bonds.

43. Fixed rate bond

A bond which has a fixed rate of interest over its entire term

44. Flat yield curve

A type of yield curve that occurs when anticipated interest rates are steady. It means that yields on short-term bonds and long-term bonds are very close.

45. Floating rate bond

This is a bond having an interest rate that is tied to a predetermined benchmark rate and is reset periodically. For example, RBI issued a floating rate savings bond (FRSB) in 2020, the interest rate of which is tied to the rate of post office's small savings scheme, the National Savings Certificate (NSC). This bond pays 0.35 percent more than NSC rate, on a semi-annual basis. As of January, 2024 the coupon on FRSB was 8.05%.

46. Foreign Bond

When a foreign firm issues bonds in the domestic market of another country, such bonds are known as foreign bonds. Such transactions take place in domestic currency.

47. Gilt

Government bonds in the U.K., India, and several other Commonwealth countries are known as gilts. Gilts are the equivalent of U.S. Treasury securities in their respective countries. The term gilt is often used informally to describe any bond that has a very low risk of default and a correspondingly low rate of return. They are called gilts because the original certificates issued by the British government had gilt edges.

48. Green Bonds

Green Bonds are bonds that raise funds for projects that provide environmental benefits, and a sustainable economy. Green includes renewable energy, sustainable resource use, clean transportation and adaptation to climate change.

49. Government bond

Debt obligation of a national government

50. Hybrid debt capital instruments

This category combines certain characteristics of equity and certain characteristics of debt.

51. Indexed Bond

A bond that pays interest payments on the basis of a particular index (say, CPI or RPI) is known as Indexed Bond or Index-linked Bond, or Inflation-Indexed bond. The Central Government of a country mostly issues this type of bond.

52. Inflation risk

The risk that a bond's returns may not keep pace with inflation

53. Interest

The amount paid by a borrower (bond issuer) to a creditor (bond holder), as compensation for the use of borrowed money

54. Interest rate Risk

The risk that a bond's price will fall when interest rate rises

55. Inverted yield curve

This situation occurs when short-term bond yields are higher than long-term bond yields.

56. Investment-grade bond

Bonds rated "BBB" or better by Standard & Poor's Corporation or a similar rating agency. The assumption is that investment-grade bonds will make prompt payment of interest and principal at maturity.

57. Junk bond

Another name for a high-yield bond. Based on the two big rating agencies, junk bonds are those with a **"Baa" rating or lower from Moody's and a rating lower than "BBB" from S&P**. Bonds with "C" rating carry a higher risk of default and a "D" rating shows that the bond is in default.

58. Letter of credit (LOC)

A commitment, usually issued by a bank, used to guarantee the payment of principal and interest on debt securities.

59. Leverage

The use of borrowed money to increase investing power

60. LIBOR (London Interbank Offered Rate)

The rate banks charge each other for short -term Eurodollar loans. LIBOR is used as the base for resetting rates on floating - rate securities.

61. Liquidation value

The amount a securities holder may receive in case of a liquidation of the issuer

62. Liquidity

The ability to trade bonds efficiently without causing major changes in their prices

63. Lockout

The period of time before an investor will begin receiving principal payments

64. Market price

The price at which a security is traded

65. Masala Bonds

Bonds issued by Indian entities in foreign countries are called Masala Bonds. Masala bonds are traded in Indian currency.

66. Maturity date

The date when the principal amount of a security becomes due and payable

67. Modified Duration

Duration adjusted to price and yield levels to represent percentage change relationship of price and yield

68. Mortgage pass-through security

A security representing a direct interest in a pool of mortgage loans. The pass-through issuer or servicer collects the payments on the loans in the pool and "passes-through" the principal and interest to the holders of the security on a pro rata basis. Mortgage pass-through securities are also called mortgage-backed securities (MBS).

69. Municipal Bond

A bond issued by a state or local government unit. In the US interest income from municipal bonds are free from federal and state income taxes. In India RBI on November 11, 2022, in its first report on municipal bonds, suggested that civic bodies must consider issuing municipal bonds to meet their funding requirements for infra structure projects. Municipal bonds are also known as 'munis'.

70. Odd lot

Block of bonds of $100,000 or less. The odd lot size can differ in different markets.

71. Offer

The price at which a seller will sell a security

72. Over-the-counter market (OTC)

A securities market that is conducted by dealers through negotiated price.

73. Par

Price equal to the face amount of a security; 100%

74. Perpetual floating-rate bond

A floating-rate bond with no stated maturity date

75. PO (Principal –only) security

In the case of a CMO, a PO tranche is created to pay the investor principal only and not interest. PO securities are priced at a deep discount from their face value.

76. Pool

A collection of mortgage loans assembled by an originator, based on which a security is issued

77. Premium

The amount by which the price of a security exceeds its principal amount

78. Prepayment

The unscheduled partial or full payment of the principal amount on a mortgage loan before it is due

79. Prepaymet risk

The risk that an investor in mortgage loans face. In a falling interest rate environment larger prepayments of mortgage loans take place, forcing the investor to reinvest at lower prevailing rates. The mortgage holder will be able to refinance his mortgage at a lower rate than the rate at which he held the previous mortgage.

80. Primary market

New issue market or market for new issue of a debt security

81. Prime rate

A commercial bank's stated reference rate for lending to most creditworthy customers. It is also called Prime lending rate.

82. Principal

The face amount of a bond, excluding accrued interest, payable at maturity

83. Private placement

Offering of new securities directly to investors at negotiated prices, without a public underwriting

84. Putable bond

A putable bond is a type of bond that gives the investor (bond holder) a right, but not an obligation, to put the bond back to the issuer before its maturity.

85. Rating

Alpha and/or numeric symbols used to give indications of the credit quality of the issuer of a bond. Globally, Standard & Poor's, Moody's and Fitch are the major rating agencies. The rating scale of S&P ranges from D to AAA, with the strongest rating being AAA. CRISIL (Credit Rating Information Services of India Limited) is the largest rating agency in India. ICRA (Investment Information and Credit Rating Agency of India Limited), CARE (Credit Analysis & Research), Fitch India, Brickwork Ratings (BWR), Onida Individual Credit Rating Agency of India (ONICRA) and SME Rating Agency of India Limited (SMERA) are the credit rating agencies in India. Unlike credit rating agencies, credit bureaus in India assign a credit score to individual borrowers based on the credit worthiness and repayment behavior. Experian, Equifax and CIBIL are three credit information bureaus in India. For example, the CIBIL score ranges from 300 to 900. The higher your score, the stronger is your financial profile when you seek a loan.

86. Real yield

For inflation – linked security, the yield based on the payment stream in constant dollars, i.e., before adjustment by the inflation index ratio

87. Redemption

The paying off or buying back of a bond by the issuer

88. Reinvestment risk

The risk that the interest income or principal repayment will have to be reinvested at a lower rate in a declining rate environment

89. Risk- Free Rate

The Risk- free rate of return is the rate of return of an investment with zero risk. The risk-free rate is hypothetical, as every investment has some risk associated with it. Treasury bills are the closest investment to being risk – free. The "real" risk-free rate is calculated by subtracting the current inflation rate from the yield of Treasury security that matches the duration of an investment.

90. Secondary Market

The secondary market is the capital market where securities are traded among investors.

91. Secured Debt

Debt backed by specific assets or revenues of the borrower

92. Settlement date

The date for the delivery of securities and payment of funds

93. Short

Borrowing and then selling securities that one does not own

94. Spread to Treasury

The difference between the yield on a fixed- income security and the yield on a Treasury security of comparable maturity

95. Stated Maturity

The last possible date on which the last payment of the longest loan may be paid

96. STRIPS

Separate Trading of Registered Interest and Principal of Securities. The U.S.Treasury Department's program under which eligible securities are authorized to be stripped into principal and interest components.

97. Subordinated debt

A type of debt that places the investor behind a company's primary creditors. In the event of bankruptcy or liquidation of the debtor, subordinated debt only has a secondary claim on repayment, after other debt has been repaid.

98. Swap

A transaction in which an investor sells one security and simultaneously buys another with the proceeds

99. Syndicate

A group of underwriters formed for the purpose of participating jointly in the initial public offering of a new security issue

100. T-bill rate

The weekly average auction rate of the three-month Treasury bill.

101. Term Sheet

The term sheet is a nonbinding agreement between the issuer and a bondholder. It lists the various features of the bond such as maturity date, coupon, interest payment, liquidation preference and convertibility.

102. Total Return

The investment performance measure of a security over a stated time period which includes coupon, interest, interest on interest, and any realised or unrealised gains or losses.

103. Trade date

The purchase or sale date of a security with settlement to be made on the settlement date

104. Tranche

A class of CMO security which has the same characteristics

105. Transfer agent

A party appointed by an issuer to maintain records of securities owners, to cancel and issue certificates and to address issues arising from lost, destroyed or stolen certificates.

106. Trustee

A bank appointed by the issuer as custodian of funds and official representative of bondholders

107. Volatility

A statistical measure known as Standard deviation of the variance of price or yield of a security over time. Volatility is low if the price does not change very much over a short period of time, and high if there is a greater change.

108. Weighted average coupon (WAC)

The weighted average interest rate of a mortgage pool that serves as collateral for a security, weighted by the size of the principal loan balances

109. Weighted average loan age (WALA)

The weighted average number of months since the date of the loan origination of the mortgages in a mortgage pass-through security pool, weighted by the size of the principal of loan balances

110. Weighted average maturity (WAM)

The weighted average number of months to the final payment of each loan backing a mortgage security, weighted by the size of the principal loan balances. It is also known as weighted average remaining maturity (WARM) and Weighted average remaining term (WART).

111. When-Issued market (W/I market)

When-Issued market refers to trading in Treasury securities prior to the time they are issued by the Treasury. Trading in W/I securities start from the day the auction is announced until the day of issue of the security. All deliveries on when –issued bonds occur on the issue day of the security.

112. Yield

The annual percentage rate of return earned on a security. Yield is a function of the coupon of a security and its purchase price (For example, if a bond's coupon is 7% and the purchase price is 100, the yield is 7% (7/100 in percentage terms).

113. Yield curve

A graphical representation of the relationship between the yield and maturity of bonds having same credit quality. This curve shows the term structure of interest rates. For example, assume a two-year bond offers a yield of 1%, a five-year bond offers a yield of 1.5%,a ten-year bond offers a yield of 2%, a twenty-year bond offers a yield of 3% and a thirty-year bond offers a yield of 3.5%. When these points are connected on a graph, they exhibit a shape of a normal yield curve.

114. Yield spread

The difference in yield between two bonds. For example if the yield on a five-year U.S Treasury bond is 3% and a ten-year Treasury bond shows a yield of 3.5%, the yield spread between the bonds is 50 basis points. Yield spread is typically expressed in "basis points". In general, the higher the risk of a bond, the higher its yield spread.

115. Yield to call

The yield on a callable security calculated by assuming that interest payments will be paid until the call date, when the security will be redeemed at the call price

116. Yield to maturity (YTM)

Yield to maturity is the total return anticipated on a bond if the bond is held to maturity. In other words, it is the internal rate of return of an investment in a bond if the investor holds the bond until maturity, with all interest receipts as scheduled and reinvested at the same rate. YTM is expressed as an annual rate.

117. Yield to worst

The lowest yield to an investor, given the potential stated calls prior to the maturity of a bond

118. Z- tranche

This is the last tranche in a CMO. The Z-tranch receives no cash payments until the previous tranches are retired. While the other tranches are outstanding, the Z-tranch receives credit for periodic interest payments that increase its face value but are not paid out. When the other tranches are retired, the Z-tranche begins to receive cash payments that include both principal and continuing interest payments.

CHAPTER 4

Equities

Equities

Equity is a term for the total ownership stake in a company after the repayment of any debt, while a share or stock describes a single unit of ownership. Equity is equal to total assets minus its total liabilities. Stocks are called equities because they represent ownership in companies. That means if you buy stocks, you're buying equities and hence you're a partial owner of the company. There are two types of equity securities: common shares and preference shares. The main difference between preferred and common stock is that preferred stock has no voting rights while common stock does. Preferred shareholders have priority over a company's income, meaning they are paid dividends before common shareholders. Common stockholders are last in the queue when it comes to company assets, which means they will be paid out after creditors, bondholders, and preferred shareholders.

1. Agent

An agent is a stock brokerage firm which executes buy/sell transactions in the stock market on behalf of an investor.

2. American Depository Receipt (ADR)

These certificates represent shares of overseas stocks listed on a US exchange. ADRs allow an investor to buy and sell overseas stocks on American stock exchanges.

3. American-style Options

Options that can be exercised any time during their life time

4. Application Supported by Blocked Amount (ASBA)

ASBA is an application containing an authorization to block the application money for an IPO issue in the bank account (Saving Account and Current Account without Overdraft facility), for subscribing to the issue. ASBA provides an alternative mode of payment in IPO issues whereby the application money remains in the investor's bank account till the finalization of the basis of allotment in the issue.

5. Ask price

Ask price or offer price is the lowest price at which the owner of the equity security is willing to sell the shares in the stock market

6. Assignment

The notification to the seller of an option by the clearing corporation that the buyer has exercised his option

7. At the money option

A stock option where the strike price is equal to the market price of the underlying stock

8. Averaging Down

Process of reducing the average cost of holding of a security by buying the security at a lower price than the previous purchase

9. Bear

A bear is an investor who expects that the market or a security is poised to go downward and may try to benefit from such downward trend.

10. Bear Market

A market in which stock prices are falling

11. Beta

A measurement of the relationship between the price of a stock and movement of the underlying stock market

12. Bid Price

The highest price a buyer of a stock is willing to pay

13. Black Tuesday

Black Tuesday, October 29, 1929, was the day when Dow Jones index fell by 12%, one of the largest one day decline, fueled by a panic sell off on Wall street.

14. Blue Chip Stocks

The shares of very large and well-recognized companies with a sound financial performance

15. Bonus Shares

Bonus shares are free additional shares that a listed company gives to their existing shareholders based on the number of shares they hold. This corporate action is carried out to distribute gains of accumulated earnings without paying cash to the shareholders. The face value of bonus shares remains the same.

16. Bottom-Up Forecast

Bottom-up forecasting is a method of estimating a company's future performance by starting with low-level company data and working up to revenue.

17. Bull

A bull is an investor who believes that the share market or a particular security will go up and hence will buy the security to benefit from future price appreciation.

18. Bull Market

A market in which stock prices are rising

19. Business Day

Any day from Monday to Friday except statutory holidays when stock markets are open for trading. It is also known as trading day.

20. Buttonwood Agreement

A written agreement between 24 stockbrokers and merchants made under a buttonwood tree in New York in 1792 that paved the way for the establishment of an official stock exchange for the United States and the beginning of an American investment community that would come to be known as "Wall Street". The agreement also gave rise to a commission system for trading stocks, setting one quarter per cent commission on the value of stocks traded.

21. Call Option

An option which gives the holder the right, but not the obligation, to buy a fixed amount of certain stock at a specified price within a fixed time period. Call options are purchased by those who anticipate that the stock will increase in price.

22. Capital Stock

Shares representing ownership of a company, including preferred and common shares

23. Cash Dividend

A dividend that is paid in Cash

24. Cash Settlement

Refers to the settlement of an option, not by delivery of the underlying shares, but by cash payment of the difference between the strike price (exercise price) and the underlying settlement price

25. Circuit Breaker

Circuit breaker is a trading curb Imposed by a stock exchange to control short-term panic selling, when market index falls to certain level. Each exchange has its own rules governing circuit breakers. Circuit breaker is used not only for the market but also for individual stocks.

26. Closing Transaction

An order to close out an existing option or futures contract

27. Commission

The fee charged by an investment advisor or broker for buying/ selling securities for a client

28. Commodities

Commodities are agricultural products and natural resources that are traded on authorized commodities exchanges.

29. Common shares or Common stock

Securities that represent part ownership in a company and generally carry voting rights. Common stock holders receive dividend payments only after preferred shareholders are paid. In the event of liquidation of a company, common shareholders are last in the queue after creditors, debtors and preferred shareholders are paid.

30. Convertible Security

A security that may be converted to other securities of the issuer, as per the terms of conversion

31. Cyclical Stocks

Cyclical shares refer to stocks of companies whose earnings fluctuate with the business cycle and are accentuated by it.

32. Daily Price Limit

The maximum price advance or decline of a security during a trading session compared to the closing price of the previous day

33. Dalal Street

Dalal Street is a street in downtown Mumbai, that houses the Bombay Stock Exchange (BSE). It received the name Dalal Street after the Bombay Stock Exchange moved there in 1874 and became the first stock exchange recognized by the Indian government in 1875. The literal translation of the word "Dalal" in Marathi is a broker or intermediary. As per history a group of five stock brokers used to conduct meetings under a banyan tree in front of Mumbai Town Hall since 1850 and later this small group moved to Dalal Street in 1874.

34. Day Order

An order that is valid for the trading session in a day

35. Defensive Stock

The stock of a company that has maintained a record of stable earnings and continuous dividend payments through period of economic downturn

36. Delist

The removal of a security's listing from a stock exchange. There may be several reasons for delisting such as bankruptcy or the failure of the company to comply with the listing requirements.

37. Delivery Month

The calendar month in which a futures contract may be settled by making or taking delivery

38. Delta

Delta is the ratio comparing the change in the price of an underlying security to the corresponding change in the price of a derivative

39. Dematerialisation

The process of converting physical shares into electronic format

40. Depository in India

A depository in India is a financial institution that holds securities such as shares and bonds in de-materialised form and facilitates trading in stock exchanges. There are two depositories in India currently: National Securities Depositories Limited (NSDL) and Central Depository Services (India) Limited (CDSL).

41. Dilution

Dilution occurs when a company issues new stock which then results in the decrease of the ownership percentage for existing shareholders.

42. Diversification

Limiting the investment risk of a portfolio by purchasing different type of securities of different companies in different sectors is known as diversification. Diversification is aimed at reducing portfolio risk by adding un-correlated stocks in the portfolio.

43. Dividend

Distribution of part of the profit of a company to holders of common stock and preferred shareholders. Most companies distribute dividends on a quarterly basis.

44. Dividend Reinvestment Plan

A method of reinvesting dividends in the additional shares of a company, which would otherwise be paid in cash to the shareholders. This method is mostly practised by mutual funds.

45. Dividend Yield

Dividend yield is the ratio of the annual dividend per share divided by the current share price. If a company pays $1 dividend per year and the current share price is $20, the dividend yield would be 5%.

46. Dividend Date

The date set by a company for distribution of dividend to its shareholders

47. Diworsification

It is the process of adding investments to a portfolio in such a way that the risk-return tradeoff of the portfolio is worsened rather than improved. This happens usually when too many assets with similar correlations are added to a portfolio without the benefit of higher returns. It results in the opposite result of diversification.

48. Dogs of the Dow

The term "Dogs of the Dow" refers to an investment strategy of buying the highest dividend paying blue chip stocks among the 30 components of the Dow, with the objective of beating the return of the Dow Jones Industrial Average (DJIA), each year. It requires rebalancing every year. The strategy's track record shows that it beat the index during the 10-year stretch that followed the financial crisis of 2008. It is a low cost strategy to achieve the return of DJIA over a long term.

49. Dollar Cost Averaging

Investing the same amount of money at regular intervals over an extended period of time, regardless of the share price. By investing a fixed amount, you purchase more shares when prices are low, and fewer shares when prices are high. This may reduce your overall average cost of investing.

50. Dot-com Bubble

Dot-com bubble refers to the period between 1995 and 2000, when investors chased internet-based start-up companies, in the hopes that such companies would provide big profits. This period is also called internet bubble. The NASDAQ index rose five times during this period, but the bubble burst in 2000, leading to a recession.

51. Dow Jones Industrial Average (DJII)

The most commonly used indicator of stock market performance in New York Stock Exchange, based on prices of 30 actively traded blue chip stocks, primarily major industrial companies. The Average is the sum of the current market price of 30 major industrial companies' stocks divided by a number that has been adjusted to take into account stocks splits and changes in stock composition.

52. Draft Red Herring Prospectus (DRHP)

A Draft Red Herring Prospectus (DRHP) is a document that introduces a new business or product to a potential investor. This document should be able to communicate the product vision and target audience to prospective investors.

53. Efficient Market

An efficient market is one in which every security's price equals its investment value at all times.

54. Employee Stock Option Plan (ESOP)

Employee stock option plan (ESOP) is an employee benefit plan that gives employees ownership in the company in the form of shares of stock. ESOP is common in US and UK companies. ESOP is intended to attract wider participation of the employees and to instill a feeling of ownership together with shareholders. Through ESOP employees also get a feeling of appreciation and compensation for their hard work.

55. Equities

Common and preferred stocks, which represent a share in the ownership of a company

56. Equity Option

An option contract that grants an investor the right to buy or sell a specified number of common stock of a company at a specified price during a specified period of time

57. Equity Price

The traded price of a share

58. Equity Value

The total value of shares traded, calculated by multiplying the total number of shares by the price per share of a security. For example if 100,000 shares of a company changed hands on a day at a price of INR 50, the equity value is 100,000 x 50 = INR 50,00,000. It is also known as the traded value.

59. European – Style Option

Options that can be exercised only on their expiration date

60. Ex Dividend Date

It is the day when the stock of a company goes ex-dividend, meaning stocks bought from that date are not entitled to the declared dividend.

61. Ex Right

The holder of the shares purchased ex rights is not entitled to the rights already declared

62. Exchange – Traded Fund (ETF)

An exchange-traded fund (ETF) is a basket of securities that tracks an underlying index. ETF can contain investments such as stocks and bonds.

63. Exercise

The act of exercising an option whereby the option holder chooses to take delivery (calls) or make delivery (puts) of the underlying security against payment of the exercise price

64. Expiration Date

The date at which an option contract expires. The option contract can't be exercised after that date.

65. Extended Trading

Extended-hours trading is trading conducted by electronic networks and is applicable mainly to the United States. It refers to stock trading that happens before or after the trading hours of the stock exchanges in the United States, such as New York stock exchange or NASDAQ. The regular trading hours of these exchanges are from 9.30am to 4.00pm EST. The before hours trading starts at 4.00am EST, but most of the trades happen between 8.00am and 9.30am. The after hours trading starts at 4.00pm but most of the trades take place before 6.30pm.

66. FAAMG Stocks

FAAMG is an acronym coined by Goldman Sachs for five top performing tech stocks in the market, namely Meta (formerly Face Book), Amazon, Apple, Microsoft and Google's Alphabet. FAAMG is also known as GAFAM.

67. FAANG Stocks

An acronym that refers to five prominent US stocks which are American technology companies: Meta (formerly Facebook), Apple, Amazon, Netflix, and Alphabet (formerly Google). These companies are among the largest stocks in the world. The term was coined by The Street's Bob Lang, and popularized by Jim Cramer on his CNBC TV show Mad Money.

68. Fill or Kill (FOK) Order

A type of equity order that requires immediate and complete execution of a trade or its cancellation

69. FMCG Stocks

FMCG refers to Fast-moving consumer goods. Such goods sell very fast at relatively lower cost. FMCG stocks are shares of those companies in the FMCG sector.

70. Follow - on Public Offer (FPO)

A follow – on public offer (FPO) refers to the issuance of additional shares to investors by a company listed on a stock exchange, after an initial public offering. Such offering is also known as secondary offering.

71. Foreign Portfolio Investment (FPI)

Foreign Portfolio Investment (FPI) refers to investments in financial assets made by an investor outside his country. FPIs are a significant factor in the Indian equity market.

72. Forensic Investing

In a forensic investing, investors look beyond the numbers on financial statements and dig deeper into the corpse of the company or a mutual fund. Many investors fail to understand financial statements and the relative footnotes because of their complexity. Forensic analysts spend time looking for specific indications of potential problems or red flags. To become a certified financial forensics, an individual must be a CPA, pass the Certified Financial Forensics (CFF) exam and meet certain requirements.

73. Front Running

Front running is the practice by market makers of dealing in equities, options, futures, and swaps to make profit based on non-pubic information before clients are given opportunity to act on such information.

74. Fundamental Analysis

Analysis of future levels of economy, industry sales and earnings, company sales and earnings and eventual forecast of likely returns from a stock. Fundamental analysis is a valuation tool used by stock analysts to determine whether a stock is over or undervalued by the market. Fundamental analysis is the analysis of financial statements of a company to interpret financial ratios, to analyze operating activities, investing activities, liquidity, solvency and profitability, for determining the fair valuation of its stock and finding if the market price is undervalued or overvalued.

75. Futures

Contracts to buy or sell securities at a future date

76. Grey Market

Grey market refers to the buying and selling of shares before they are issued on the official stock exchange.

77. Grey Market Premium (GMP)

Grey Market Premium (GMP) is the premium amount at which an IPO issue is traded in the grey market before it is listed in the exchange.

78. Growth Stock

The shares of companies that have exhibited better-than-average growth over recent years and are expected to show such growth going forward

79. Hedge Fund

A hedge fund is an investment partnership between a fund manager and investors to pool their money together into the fund.

80. Herd Instinct

Herd instinct is an inborn tendency to associate with others and follow the group behaviour. This is used very much in the financial sector to refer to investor behaviour. It is an intent by investors to copy the action of other investors.

81. Large Cap

Large Cap stocks in the U.S mean the stocks of companies with market values greater than $10 billion.

82. High Net-worth Individuals (HNIs)

The term high net-worth individuals, popularly referred to as HNIs, is not defined anywhere. In common parlance this refers to a class of individuals who have an investable surplus of INR 5 crores or a net-worth of above INR 25 crores.

83. Income Stock

A common stock with a good track record of dividend payments and which offers a dividend yield higher than general market

84. Index

A market index is a hypothetical portfolio representing a segment of the financial market. In India the popular indexes include the SENSEX and NIFTY. In the US market the popular ones are Dow Jones, S&P 500, and NASDAQ.

85. Inflation

An overall increase in prices of goods and services, usually measured by the percentage change in the Consumer Price Index (CPI). Wholesale Price Index (WPI) is also a popular inflation index.

86. Initial Public Offering (IPO)

The first- time issue of shares to the public by a company

87. Inside Information

Non-public information regarding the business affairs of a company, that could have an influence on the share price of that company should the information be made public.

88. Insider

All directors and senior officials of a company and those who are presumed to be in possession of inside information

89. Insider Trading

There are two types of insider trading. The first type occurs when insiders trade in the stock of their company. In such cases they should report the transactions to the appropriate securities commissions. The second type of insider trading happens when anyone trades stocks based on non-public material information. This type of insider trading is illegal. In various countries there are stringent punishments for such activities.

90. International Securities Identification Number (ISIN)

This is a system to identify a specific security, introduced in 1981 by the Group of 30 (G30). An ISIN code is a 12-digit alphanumeric number – the first two letters refer to the country in which the company is based, the next nine digits identify the specific security, and the final character is a check digit. For example the ISIN code of State Bank of India is INE062A01012. In India SEBI has entrusted the task of issuing ISIN code to National Securities Depository Limited (NSDL) for issuing ISIN to various securities. For the government securities, the allotment of the ISIN code is regulated by the Reserve Bank of India (RBI).The United States and Canada use the CUSIP numbering system that is similar to ISIN.

91. Intrinsic Value

Intrinsic value is the perceived or calculated value of a security or an investment and is used in fundamental analysis and the options markets. The discrepancy between market price and an analyst's estimated intrinsic value becomes a measure for investing opportunity. In the case of options, the difference between the current market price of the underlying security and the strike price of the option is considered as the intrinsic value. When the intrinsic value is positive, it is called an In –the – money option.

92. Investment Advisor

A person who provides investment advice to clients

93. Investment Dealer

Securities firms that employ investment advisors to work with retail and institutional clients

94. January Barometer

The term "January Barometer" refers to the notion held by US traders that the investment performance of the S&P 500 index in January can predict its performance for the rest of the year. For example, the proponents believe that if the index produces positive return in January, it can produce positive return for the year and vice versa.

95. January Effect

The term "January Effect" is a hypothesis that there is seasonal anomaly in the stock market where stock prices in January rise more than in any other month in the year. This is due to the fact that investors resort to tax loss selling in December and buy back shares in January.

96.Limit Order

An order to buy or sell stock at a specified price

97. Liquidity

The ease with which a security can be bought or sold in the market. Liquidity is one of the most important characteristics of a good market.

98. Listed Stock

Shares of a company that are traded on a stock exchange. Issuers of security have to pay fees to the exchange and comply with the rules and regulations of the exchange to maintain the listing.

99. Listing Application

The document that an issuer has to submit to the exchange for listing. It includes information regarding the company's activities, plans, management, and finances

100. Long Position

A term that denotes the ownership of securities. For example if you are long 100 shares of ABC, this means that you own 100 shares of ABC company.

101. Maharatna company

Central Public Sector Enterprises in India are categorized into three groups by Government of India. They are Maharatna, Navaratna, and Miniratna. This categorization is done on different criteria. The eligibility criteria for granting Maharatna status are : (1) Having Navratna status, (2) Listed on Indian stock exchange with minimum prescribed public shareholding under SEBI regulations, (3) An average annual net profit after tax of more than Rs. 5,000 crore during the last 3 years, (4) An average annual Turnover of Rs. 25,000 crore for 3 years, or the average annual Net worth of Rs. 15,000 crore for 3 years, and (5) Must bear global presence/ international operations. A Maharatna Company enjoys more autonomy in terms of financial decisions. Maharatna Companies in India have the advantages which help them operate globally and have the freedom to invest up to 15% of their net worth in a project. These companies are crucial to the Indian economy. At the end of 2023, there were 13 Maharatna companies in India, (1) Bharat Petroleum Corporation Limited (BPCL), (2) Steel Authority of India Limited (SAIL), (3) Oil and Natural Gas Corporation (ONGC), (4) Indian Oil Corporation Limited (IOCL), (5) Bharat Heavy Electricals Limited (BHEL), (6) Rural Electrification Corporation (REC), (7) Hindustan Petroleum Corporation Limited (HPCL), (8) Coal India Limited (CIL), (9) National Thermal Power Corporation (NTPC), (10) Gas Authority of India Limited (GAIL), (11) Power Finance Corporation, (12) Power Grid Corporation of India, and (13) Oil India Limited.

102. Margin Account

An account of a client with a securities dealer that uses credit from the dealer to buy a security.

103. Market Capitalisation

It is the total value of the issued shares of a public limited company. It is calculated by multiplying the total number of outstanding shares by the share price.

104. Market Order

An order to buy or sell a share at the prevailing market price

105. Mid Cap Stocks

Mid Cap stocks in the U.S are the stocks of companies with market values between $3 to $10 billion. In the Indian market, a mid-cap stock has a market capitalization ranging from Rs. 5,000 crores to Rs. 20,000 crores.

106. Miniratna company

Miniratna companies are the ones with pre-tax profit of Rs. 30 crores or more in at least one of the three years and have also a net worth eligible to be considered for granting Miniratna status. There are two categories within Miniratna companies, Category I and Category II. Category I companies are the companies that have made a profit continuously in the last three years, have made a net profit of INR 30 crores or more in one of the three previous years. Category 2 companies are those with the power to incur capital expenditure on new projects, modernisation, purchase of equipment etc., without Government approval upto Rs. 250 crore or equal to 50 % of the net worth, whichever is less. In category 1, there are 62 companies and in category 2, there are 11 companies.

Category 1 Companies (30 companies given below)

1. Airports Authority of India	16. Garden Reach Shipbuilders & Engineers Limited
2. Antrix Corporation Limited	17. Goa Shipyard Limited
3. Balmer Lawrie & Co. Limited	18. Hindustan Copper Limited
4. Bharat Coking Coal Limited	19.. HLL Lifecare Limited
5. Bharat Dynamics Limited	20. Hindustan Newsprint Limited
6. BEML Limited	21. Hindustan Paper Corporation Limited
7. Bharat Sanchar Nigam Limited	22. Housing & Urban Development Corporation Limited
8. Bridge & Roof Company (India) Limited	23. HSCC (India) Limited
9. Central Warehousing Corporation	24. India Tourism Development Corporation Limited
10. Central Coalfields Limited	25. Indian Rare Earths Limited
11. Central Mine Planning & Design Institute Limited	26. Indian Railway Catering & Tourism Corporation Limited
12. Chennai Petroleum Corporation Ltd.	27. Indian Railway Finance Corpn. Ltd.
13. Cochin Shipyard Limited	28. India Renewable Energy Development Agency Limited

14. EdCIL (India) Limited	29. India Trade Promotion Organization
15. Kamarajar Port Limited	30. IRCON International Limited

Category 2 (Given below are 10 companies)

1. Artificial Limbs Manufacturing Corp. of India	6. Ferro Scrap Nigam Ltd
2. Broadcast Engineering Consultants India Ltd.	7. Indian Medicine Pharmaceutical Corp. Ltd.
3. Central Railside Warehouse Co. Ltd.	8. Mecon Ltd.
4. Engineering Projects (India) Ltd.	9. National Film Development Corp. Ltd.
5. FCI Aravali Gypsum & Minerals (India) Ltd.	10. Rajasthan Electronics & Instruments Ltd.

107. Muhurat Trading

Muhurat Trading is an event unique to the Indian stock market. It is a one hour trading session held in BSE and NSE on the evening of Diwali day, as announced by the exchanges. The word 'muhurat' means an auspicious time in Hindu customs. Muhurat is the time when planets are aligned favourably to ensure positive results. According to beliefs, people trading during this one hour have a better chance of earning wealth and prosperity throughout the year. People prefer buying stocks during this hour as a token of Goddess Laxmi, the Goddess of wealth, fortune, power, beauty, prosperity and fertility.

108. Mutual Fund

A mutual fund is an investment vehicle consisting of a portfolio of stocks, bonds, or other securities, managed by a professional investment manager.

109. Naked Option

A naked option is created when the option seller does not own the underlying security

110. Naked Short Selling

Naked short selling is an illegal practice of short selling shares which are not existing. Ordinarily traders have to borrow shares before they sell it short. Naked short selling was made illegal after the 2008 financial crisis. Despite that, naked short selling continues to take place.

111. NASDAQ

National Association of Securities Dealers Automated Quotations system, which is owned and operated by the National Association of Securities Dealers in the U.S. NASDAQ is a computerized system that provides brokers and dealers with price quotations for securities traded over-the-counter as well as for many New York Stock Exchange listed securities.

112. Net Worth

The difference between a company's assets and liabilities. It is also called Shareholder's equity for a company.

113. New Issue

The issue of a stock or bond by a company for the first time

114. New Listing

An issue of a security that is newly added to the list of tradable security in an exchange

115. Odd lot

A number of shares that are less than a regular trading unit decided by a particular stock exchange

116. One-Sided Market

A market that has only buy orders or only sell orders

117. Open Interest

The net open positions of a futures or option contract

118. Open Order

An order that remains open in the system for more than a day

119. Option

The right, but not the obligation, to buy or sell certain securities at a specified price within a specified time. There are mainly two types of Options – Call option and Put option. Call option gives the holder the right to buy the security and the put option gives the holder the right to put (sell) the security.

120. Option Premium

An option premium is the income received by an investor who sells an option contract. In the case of buying an option, the premium is the amount paid by the purchaser to the seller of the option. The premium has two basic components: Intrinsic value and time value. Intrinsic value is equal to the difference between the strike price (exercise price) and the asset's current market price, when the difference is positive. For example, suppose an investor buys a call option for ABC company, with a strike price of INR 45 and if the stock's market price is INR 50, the option has an intrinsic value of INR 5 (50 -45). Time Value refers to the portion of an option's premium that is attributable to the amount of time remaining until the expiration of the option contract. For example, if the option premium is INR 7 in the above example, the Time Value of the option can be inferred as INR 2 (7 – 5). The implied volatility of the underlying security is also imbedded in the option premium.

121. Option Writer

The seller of an option contract may be required to deliver the security covered by the option in the case of a call option or to purchase the security covered by the option in the case of a put option, before the expiry of the option contract.

122. Over-the-Counter (OTC) Market

The market maintained by security dealers for securities not listed on a stock exchange. Almost all bonds and debentures are traded over-the-counter market.

123. Penny Stock

Low priced speculative stock selling at less than one dollar a share. In India, penny stocks are traded for Rs.10 or less.

124. Portfolio

Portfolio is a collection of investments. The investments include various types of securities (For example, a portfolio may include money market securities, bonds, common stocks, real estate, private equities, hedge funds and other types of investments).

125. Preferred Share

Preferred shares are a type of company stock with dividends that are paid to shareholders before common stock dividends are paid out. Preferred shares usually do not enjoy voting rights.

126. Price/Book Value

The relation between the market price of a stock and its book value (stockholders' equity per share). For example, if a stock's market price is INR 150 and its book value is INR 75, the Price/Book value is 2 (150 divided by 75).

127. Price-Earnings (P/E) Ratio

This ratio is a measure of how many times the actual or the anticipated annual earnings a stock is trading at. It is calculated by dividing the current market price of a common stock by the latest 12- month earnings per share. For example, if stock XYZ is trading at INR 100, and the stock's latest annual earnings per share is INR 10, XYZ is trading at 10 PE.

128. Price to Free Cashflow

This is a measure of how many times the free cash flow a stock is trading. It is calculated by dividing the market capitalization by the free cash flow. It is a valuation metric to indicate a company's ability to continue operating.

129. Price/Earnings-to-Growth (PEG) Ratio

PEG ratio is a method used to value common stocks through a trade off between its price, earnings per share, and the expected growth of earning.

PEG Ratio of a common stock = P/E Ratio / Annual EPS Growth rate

In general, a PEG ratio less than 1 means the stock is undervalued and a ratio over 1 means the stock is overvalued.

130. Price –to – Sales (P/S) Ratio

The Price - to – Sales ratio is a valuation ratio that compares a company's stock price to its revenues. The ratio shows how much investors are willing to pay per Rupee of sales. It is calculated by dividing the stock price by sales per share.

131. Primary Market

When a company issues new stock directly to investors (buyer), it is said to be a primary market issue. The company receives funds directly from the sale of stocks in a primary market.

132. Private Placement

The private offering of a security to a small group of investors. In such case the resale of the security is limited.

133. Prospectus

A legal document describing the terms and conditions of securities being offered for sale to the public.

134. Put Option

A put option is a contract that gives the holder the right to put (sell) a specified number of shares at a stated price during a fixed time period. Put options are purchased by those who anticipate a decline in the price of a stock.

135. Qualified Institutional Placement (QIP)

It is a way to raise capital by listed companies by selling equity to qualified institutional investors. It is common in India for listed companies to raise capital this way without going through the legal paperwork required by market regulators.

136. Real Estate Investment Trust (REIT)

Real Estate Investment Trust (REIT) is an exchange-traded fund that invests the majority of its assets in equity REIT securities and related derivatives. Equity REITs primarily own commercial real estate, namely shopping centers, apartments, and industrial buildings. Because of the trust structure REITs offer tax advantages to investors.

137. Redeemable Security

A security that gives the issuer a right to redeem or call the security at a certain price within a set time period.

138. Retractable Security

A security that has an option feature for the holder to require the issuer to redeem it, subject to certain terms and conditions

139. Secondary Market

Subsequent to the sale of stock in a primary market, people buy and sell these shares of stock, trading among themselves in the secondary market (for example, on the Bombay Stock Exchange or on the New York Exchange).

140. Settlement

Settlement is the process by which the seller delivers the security to the buyer and the buyer makes payment for the security.

141. Settlement Date

The date when a buyer of the security must pay for the purchase and the seller must deliver the security. Different markets have different settlement rules. Currently, Indian stock exchanges follow T+1 days settlement cycle, i.e, settlement of funds and securities takes place one business day after the day the order is executed. The settlement cycle for US stocks is T+2. However, the settlement cycle moves to T+1 on 28th May 2024.

142. Share Certificate

A paper certificate that represents the number of shares an investor owns

143. Short Selling

Short selling is a trading strategy whereby the seller sells a security that he does not own or a security that he borrows.

144. Social Stock Exchange (SSE)

Social Stock Exchange (SSE) is a novel concept introduced in India. Such a bourse is meant to raise capital for social enterprises. Its benefit is better utilization of funds by tracking the utilization of funds. There will be separate segments for SSEs in NSE and BSE. SSEs operate under the guidelines of SEBI.

145. SOTP Valuation

Sum of the Parts (SOTP) valuation is a method of valuing a company by separately valuing each segment of its business or subsidiary and then adding them together to find the total value of the company.

146. Spread

Difference between the bid and ask price of a stock

147. Strategic Asset Allocation (SAA)

Strategic asset allocation is a portfolio strategy whereby the investor sets target allocations for various asset classes and rebalances the portfolio periodically. The target allocations are based on factors such as the investor's risk tolerance, time horizon, and investment objectives.

148. Stock Dividend

Sometimes a corporation's management decides to forgo a cash dividend but pay a stock dividend instead. For example, if a 5% stock dividend is declared, the owner of 500 shares receives 25 additional shares.

149. Stock Split

A Stock Split is similar to stock dividend but differs in both magnitude and accounting treatment. In this case par value is adjusted appropriately and the surplus account left unchanged. For example, if an INR 2- par stock is split " 2 for 1", the holder of 100 old shares will receive 200 new INR 1- par shares. A stock split increases the number of shares and decreases the par value per share. A **Reverse Stock Split** reduces the number of shares and increases the par value per share.

150. Tactical Asset Allocation (TAA)

Tactical asset allocation is an active portfolio management strategy that shifts the percentage of assets held in various categories to take advantage of market pricing anomalies or strong market sectors.

151. Technical Analysis

A method of analysing stocks based on historical stock prices and other trading variables

152. Ticker Symbol

A system of letters used to identify a stock. For example, the ticker symbol of State Bank of India in NSE is **SBIN** and the ticker for Tesla Inc in NASDAQ is **TSLA.**

153. Top-Down Forecasting

Top-down forecasting is a method of estimating a company's future performance by starting with high-level market data and working down to company's revenue.

154. Treasury Stock

Treasury stock, otherwise known as Treasury shares, refers to previously outstanding stock that is bought back from stockholders by the issuing company. The result is that the number of outstanding shares decreases and these shares are not counted for the distribution of dividends or the calculation of earnings per share (EPS).

155. Underwriters

Underwriters are financial institutions such as banks, that pledge to buy all the unsold shares in an issue of new shares.

156. Volatility

Volatility is simply how fast the price of a stock is moving up or down. It is a statistical measure of the dispersion of returns for a given security

157. Volatile Stocks

Stocks that are affected by stock market fluctuations in terms of price and volume

158. Volume

The number of shares traded during a given period for a stock or an entire exchange

159. Warrants

Warrants are issued by corporations as sweeteners as part of new common stock issues. Warrants give their holders an option to purchase the corporation's securities, usually its common stock, at a stated price within a stated period. In simple terms warrant is a call option. The warrant holder has no voting rights and receives no dividend income. Most warrants are protected against stock splits and stock dividends.

160. Whistleblower

A whistleblower (also written as whistle-blower) is a person, normally an employee, who reveals information about activities within a private or public organization, that is deemed illegal, immoral, fraudulent, wrong-doing, or illicit.

CHAPTER 5

Financial Statements

Financial Statements

Financial statements are written records that show the business activities and the financial performance of a company. The income statement, balance sheet, statement of cashflows and statement of changes in equity are the important components of a financial statement. Financial statements are initially audited by the company's internal audit department and then external auditors (accountants) to ensure accuracy. The statements are subject to audit by government agencies also to ensure accuracy for tax, financing and investment purposes. This chapter provides the glossary applicable to various terms used in financial statements.

A. ASSETS

1. Accounts Receivable

The amount of money owed to the company by its customers for the sale of its products and services

2. Cash and Cash equivalents

Liquid assets, which include cash held in bank accounts, short-term investments, Treasury bills, and other money market instruments.

3. Fixed Assets

Fixed assets are assets purchased for long-term use, such as land, building, and equipment.

4. Inventory

Inventory is the goods on hand of a company, which it intends to sell during the course of its business. Inventory may include finished goods, work in progress and raw materials on hand for production.

5. Investments

Investments are assets held for future growth, and not used for operations.

6. Prepaid Expenses

These are expenses that have been paid in advance. These expenses are recorded as an asset because the value of them has not yet been recognized.

7. Property, Plant and Equipment

Property, plant, and equipment are the long-term assets owned by a company. They are mostly fixed assets such as trucks, machinery, factories, and land.

8. Trademarks, Patents and Goodwill

These are intangible assets that can't be physically touched but have future benefits.

B. BALANCE SHEET

1. Balance Sheet

A balance sheet is a financial statement that reports a company's assets, liabilities and shareholder equity at a specific point in time.

2. Assets

An asset is anything that has current or future economic value to a business. Assets include everything controlled and owned by a company. Examples include patents, machinery, and investments.

3. Liabilities

In financial accounting, a liability is defined as a future sacrifice of economic benefits that an entity is obliged to make to other entities as a result of past transactions. Examples are bank loans, mortgages, unpaid bills or any sum of money that is owed to someone else.

C. CASHFLOW STATEMENT (CFS)

1. Cashflow Statement

This is a statement showing how a company's operations are running, where its money is coming from, and how money is being spent. CFS gives an insight into the company's financial footing.

2. Financing Activities

Financing activities include debt issuance, equity issuance, stock repurchase, loans, dividends paid, and repayment of debt.

3. Investing Activities

This includes any sources and uses of cash from a company's investments into the long-term future of a company, including purchase or sale of an asset.

4. Operating Activities

Sources and uses of cash from running the business and selling its products or services

D. FINANCIAL ANALYSIS

1. Capital Asset Pricing Model (CAPM)

Capital Asset Pricing Model (CAPM) is a mathematical model that estimates the return on an asset based on its riskiness relative to the rest of the market.

2. Earnings Before Interest and Taxes (EBIT)

Earnings before interest and taxes (EBIT) is an indicator of a company's profitability. It is calculated by deducting expenses from revenue, but excluding interest and taxes.

3. Earnings Before Interest, Taxes, Depreciation and Amortization (EBITDA)

EBITDA is a widely used measure of corporate profitability. It is calculated by deducting interest, taxes, depreciation and amortization from revenue.

4. Enterprise Resource Planning (ERP)

ERP is a platform that businesses use to manage and integrate essential parts of their business. ERP software is used for this purpose.

5. Environmental, Social, and Governance Criteria (ESG)

ESG refers to a set of criteria a company uses to safeguard environment. Socially conscious investors use this for analysing stocks for investments.

6. Feasibility Study

Feasibility study is the study of the practicality of a project, based on the analysis of various factors, such as economic, legal, operational, and time horizon.

7. Future Value (FV)

Future value is the value of a current asset at a future date, based on an assumed rate of growth.

8. Present Value (PV)

Present Value is the current value of a future sum of money or a future stream of cashflows, at a given rate of return. Future cashflows are discounted at the discount rate and higher the discount rate, lower the present value. Deciding the appropriate discount rate is the key factor in discounting future cashflows.

E. GENERALLY ACCEPTED ACCOUNTING PRINCIPLES (GAAP)

It is a set of rules governing the preparation of financial statements by United States companies. International companies may use a similar but different set of rules known as International Financial Reporting Standards (IFRS).

F. LIABILITIES

1. Accounts Payable

Bills due as part of the normal course of business of a company. Examples are utility bills, rent, and amounts due for buying raw materials.

2. Bank Debt

Debt owed to banks

3. Dividends Payable

These are dividends declared by the company but not yet paid

4. Long -Term Debt

Long term loans payable by the company

5. Taxes owed

Unpaid taxes to the government

6. Wages owed

Unpaid wages to employees

G. SHAREHOLDERS' EQUITY

Shareholders' equity (also known as stockholders' equity) is a company's total assets minus its total liabilities. The four categories of Shareholders' equity are common shares, preferred shares, paid-in capital and retained earnings.

H. STATEMENT OF CHANGES IN SHAREHOLDERS' EQUITY

This includes the beginning equity (equity at the end of the last period), plus net income earned during a given period, minus dividends paid, plus/minus other comprehensive income.

CHAPTER 6

Corporate Finance

Corporate Finance

Corporate finance is that branch of finance that deals with the sources of raising capital, the capital structure of corporations, the actions that managers take to increase the shareholders' value, and the methods used to allocate financial resources efficiently. Thus, Corporate finance refers to planning, developing and controlling the capital structure of a business. The five main areas of Corporate Finance are **capital budgeting, capital structure, working capital management, corporate governance, and risk management.** The key terms used in corporate finance are discussed below:

1. Angel Investor

An angel investor is a high net-worth investor who invests directly in a start-up expecting a high return upon the sale of the company. Angel investing is very risky with the probability of total loss.

2. Annual Percentage Rate (APR)

Annual percentage rate (APR) is the total cost of borrowing in an year, including the fees and other costs. It is expressed as a percentage of the principal amount borrowed.

3. Asset

An asset is a resource with economic value that an individual corporation owns with the objective of earning a future benefit. The various types of assets are discussed under the chapter 'Financial Statements'.

4. Acid -Test Ratio

Acid -test ratio, also known as quick ratio, compares a company's most short-term assets to its most short-term liabilities to see if a company has enough short-term assets to pay its immediate liabilities.

5. Bankruptcy

Bankruptcy is a legal process involving a business that is unable to repay its outstanding debts. The bankruptcy process begins with a petition filed by a debtor. All of the assets of the debtor will be evaluated and the assets may be used to repay a portion of the outstanding debts.

6. Balance Sheet

Balance Sheet is a financial statement that reports the assets, liabilities and the shareholder's equity of a company. The Balance sheet along with other important financial statements such as income statement and cashflow statement are used in the fundamental analysis and calculation of financial ratios.

CHAPTER 7

Major Stock Market Indices

Methods of Calculating Stock Market Indices

We use a thermometer to check our body temperature. Similarly, in finance, a stock index, or a stock market index is an index that measures a stock market. Stock market index is used to measure the current stock price level with past prices to calculate the performance of a stock market. The Dow Jones Transportation Index is considered the world's first stock index, published by Charles Dow, in 1884. The average was calculated by adding the price of 11 transportation stocks in the U.S, including nine railway companies and dividing them by the number of stocks. There are mainly three commonly used methods for the calculation of index:

1. Equal – Weighted Index

This method uses equal weight for all stocks in the index. So, if an index was made up of 20 companies, each one would account for 5% of the index.

2. Market – Cap Weighted Index

In this method, the market cap of the stocks in the index is used for the index calculation. So, larger companies have a bigger weighting in the index.

3. Price – Weighted Index

In this method, the value of the index is calculated by adding the prices of each stock in the index and dividing them by the total number of stocks. Stock with a higher price is given more weight which has a greater influence on the performance of the index.

GLOBAL STOCK MARKET INDICES

All stock markets have several indices to measure their performances. Given below are the most popular indices of some key markets:

CHINA

1. Hang Seng Index (HSI)

The Hang Seng Index (**HSI**) is the benchmark stock market index for the Hong Kong Stock Exchange. It is a weighted index of the largest companies that trade on the Hong Kong exchange.

2. Shanghai Stock Exchange Composite Index (SSE)

The Shanghai Stock Exchange Composite Index (SSE) tracks all stocks traded on the Shanghai Stock Exchange. It is a weighted index launched on Oct.13, 1995.

3.Shanghai Shenzhen CSI 300. Index (CSI 300)

This index is designed to replicate the performance of the top 300 stocks traded in the Shanghai and Shenzhen stock exchanges and is weighted for market capitalization. The index was introduced in 2005.

GERMANY

DAX 30

German Stock Index DAX 30 consists of the 30 major German companies trading on the Frankfurt Stock Exchange. DAX 30 was launched on 30 December 1987 and is calculated through Xetra, an electronic trading system, using a free-float methodology based on a measure of the average trading volume.

INDIA

1. BSE Sensex

The BSE Sensitive index (BSE30) of equity share prices comprise 30 large capitalisation stocks traded on the Bombay Stock Exchange, considering the number of trades and the average value of shares traded per day as a percentage of total number of outstanding shares. The index was launched in 1986 with a base year 1978-79. The formula for calculating Sensex is :

Sensex = (total free float market capitalisation / base market capitalisation) * Base Index value.

2. Multi Commodity Exchange of India -MCX

Commodities traded on MCX are (1) Bullion: Gold, Silver. (2) Agriculture commodities: Black pepper, castor seed, crude palm oil, cardamom, cotton, mentha oil, rubber, palmolein, and (3) Energy: Natural gas, crude oil. MCX iCOMDEX is the leading index in MCX.

3. NIFTY 50

The NIFTY 50 is a benchmark Indian stock market index that represents the weighted average of 50 largest companies listed on the National Stock Exchange. The index was founded on 21 April 1997. The calculation is based on Capitalisation weighted methodology.

JAPAN

1. Nikkei 225

The Nikkei 225 or the Nikkei index is a stock market index for the Tokyo Stock Exchange (TSE). It is a price-weighted index. The Nikkei measures the performance of 225 large, public owned companies in Japan from different industrial sectors. The calculation of the index started on 9 July 1950.

2. Tokyo Stock Price Index (TOPIX)

Tokyo Stock Price Index (TOPIX) is another popular benchmark of the Japanese stock market. TOPIX is a free-float adjusted market capitalization –weighted index. TOPIX shows the measure of current market capitalization, assuming that the market capitalization as of the base date (January 4, 1968) is 100.

KOREA

1. KOSPI

The Korea Composite Stock Price Index (KOSPI) is the major stock market index of South Korea. The index was launched in 1983 with a base value of 100 as of January 4, 1980. The KOSPI is calculated as current market capitalization divided by the base market capitalization. KOSPI index has currently 928 constituents.

2. KOSPI 200

The KOSPI 200 index consists of 200 big companies listed on the South Korean Stock Exchange. It is calculated as current market capitalization divided by the base market capitalization as of January 4, 1980.

UNITED KINGDOM

1. FTSE 100. Index

The Financial Times Stock Exchange 100 Index, also known as FTSE 100 Index, FTSE 100 or "Footsie", is a share index of 100 companies listed on the London Stock Exchange with highest market capitalisation. It is a market capitalization weighted index. The index was founded in 1984.

2. FTSE All-Share Index

The FTSE All –Share Index is a capitalization – weighted index, comprising about 600 companies traded on the London Stock Exchange.The base date of the index is April 10, 1962.

UNITED STATES

In the United States there are approximately 5,000 stock indices. The three most widely followed and popular indices are the S&P 500, Dow Jones Industrial Average and NASDAQ Composite.

1. The S&P 500

The Standard & Poor's 500 Index (commonly known as the S&P 500) is an index comprising 500 of the top companies in the U.S. Stocks are chosen primarily by capitalization but other factors including liquidity, public float, sector, financial viability and trading history are also taken into consideration. The S&P 500 Index represents about 80% of the total value of the U.S stock market. This index is a market-weighted index.

2. The Dow Jones Industrial Average

The Dow Jones Industrial Average (DJIA) is one of the oldest, most popular, and most frequently used index in the world. It includes the stocks of 30 of the largest and most influential companies in the United States. The DJIA is a price-weighted index. More over it is representative of the blue-chip, dividend-value market. DJIA was first introduced on May 26, 1896.

3. The NASDAQ Composite Index

The Nasdaq composite index is a market capitalization weighted index of more than 3,700 stocks listed on the Nasdaq stock exchange. This is a highly technology weighted index.

CHAPTER 8

Alternative Investments – A Brief Note

ALTERNATIVE INVESTMENTS

An alternative investment is a financial asset that does not fall into one of the conventional investment categories. Conventional categories include stocks, bonds, and cash.

Alternative investments include private equity, venture capital, hedge funds, managed futures, art antiques, commodities, and derivative contracts. Real estate is also often classified as an alternative investment. Alternative investments are somewhat illiquid and subject to fewer regulations from regulatory authorities. Traditionally alternative investments were aimed at accredited investors. However, they have become accessible to retail investors through alternative funds. Most alternative investments are held by institutional investors, or high net-worth individuals due to the complex nature, illiquidity, higher risk and lack of regulation. Such investments have high minimum investment amounts and high fee structures. It is essential that investors conduct extensive due diligence when looking at alternative investments. Alternative investments have a low correlation to standard asset classes. For this reason, alternative assets are used for portfolio diversification. Because of this, many institutional portfolios allocate a small percentage of its assets to alternative investments. A discussion of alternative investments and the terms associated with alternative investments are given in subsequent chapters.

CHAPTER 9

Private Equity

Private Equity

Private equity is an alternative investment class that invests in or acquires private companies that are not listed on a public stock exchange. Investors in this asset class are usually required to commit large amount of capital for years. For this reason, access to such investments is limited to institutions and individuals with high net-worth.

1. Absolute Return

Absolute return is the return a private equity deal achieves over a certain period of time, considering the appreciation or depreciation of the deal's value.

2. Accelerator

An accelerator is program to assist a start-up company to grow to be a successful company. Generally, an accelerator will provide the start-up with office space, some capital in return for equity in the company, and assistance for a period of time.

3. Accredited Investor

An "accredited investor" is a person or entity that meets certain requirements as per securities regulation and meets certain net worth requirements for investment in private equity. Accredited investor is also known as certified investor.

4. Acquisition

An acquisition is the purchase of 50% or more of a company's outstanding voting stock. An acquisition also happens when an investor purchases substantially all of the assets of the company. The purpose of an acquisition is either strategic or financial. In a strategic acquisition an operating company purchases another company for the purpose of advancing its business strategy. In a financial acquisition, a financial buyer acquires a company in order to improve its financial performance and later sell the company at a profit.

5. Acquisition Facility

A loan provided by a bank to a private equity fund / firm, the proceeds of which are utilized to finance the acquisition of the investee company.

6. Advisory Committee

This is a group of Limited Partners in a fund selected by the General Partner to advise it on matters relating to the fund

7. Alpha

In private equity, Alpha is the value added by the fund manager's skill.

8. Alternative Assets

Alternative assets are non-traditional asset classes, such as private equity, hedge funds, and real estate. As alternative assets are more riskier than traditional assets, they should, in theory, generate higher returns for investors.

9. Angel Investor

An angel investor is a high net-worth investor who invests directly in a start-up expecting a high return upon the sale of the company. Angel investing is very risky with the probability of total loss.

10. Annual Meeting

For a private equity fund, the annual meeting is an event where the general partner (GP) presents the performance of the fund to the limited partners.

11. Antitrust Laws

Antitrust laws, also called competition laws, are statutes to protect consumers from predatory business practices. Such laws are aimed at encouraging competition by limiting the market power of any particular firm. This law ensures that mergers and acquisitions don't overly concentrate market power or form monopolies. Each country has its own antitrust laws. In India the Competition Commission of India is responsible for the enforcement of Competition Act.

12. Asset Allocation

Asset allocation refers to the allocation of portfolio assets across different asset classes.

13. Asset – Based Lending

Lending secured by the assets of the borrowing compan

14. Asset Class

Cash, bonds, equities, and alternative assets are the common asset classes.

15. Asset Stripping

The process of buying an undervalued company with a view to selling off its individual parts for a profit. The individual parts of the company, such as plant, machinery, or a division may be more valuable than the company as a whole due to poor management or other economic reasons.

16. Assets Under Management (AUM)

Assets under management refers to the total amount of funds under the management of an asset manager.

17. Benchmark

Benchmark is a reference index against which the performance of a private equity fund is compared.

18. Beta

Beta is a measure of a security's sensitivity to the movements in the underlying market.

19. Book Runner

The book running manager (book runner) in an IPO runs the process of collection of applications for the IPO and decides with the company the IPO price. The book runner is a member of the underwriting syndicate for the IPO.

20. Break-Up Fee

Break-up fee is a fee paid as compensation to a buyer who has entered into an agreement to purchase a company, should another buyer come forward and offer a higher price before the transaction closes.

21. Bridge Financing (Bridge Loan)

Bridge financing, otherwise called bridge loan, is a short-term financing given by a group of investors to a company, until the company is able to raise capital in the next round. Bridge financing may be structured as convertible debt.

22. Business Angel

An affluent individual who provides capital for a business startup, usually in exchange for convertible debt or ownership equity.

23. Buy-and-Build Strategy

A strategy in which a private equity firm buys a company in a particular industry as a platform and adds additional companies in that sector. It then merges those companies into a larger entity to create synergies and increase the group value.

24. Buyout

A buyout is a transaction whereby a private equity firm uses debt funds to acquire control of a company. It is known as a "leveraged buyout".

25. Buyout Firm

A firm that acquires a controlling interest in a company.

26. Capital Call

Capital call is a notification by a private equity fund manager (GP) to the limited partner (LP) to pay a portion of the committed capital on a set date. Capital calls are made in installments and not at once.

27. Capital Commitment

An investor in a private equity fund commits a certain amount of capital to invest in the fund. Committed capital is not drawn at once but over a period only, usually over a period of 5 – 10 years.

28. Capital Distribution

These are the returns that an investor in a private equity fund receives. The returns are in the form of income and capital gain realized from investments, less expenses and liabilities.

29. Captive Fund

A private equity fund that is tied to a larger organization, typically a bank, insurance company or a corporation.

30. Carried Interest

Carried interest is the share in the profits of a fund that the general partner is entitled to. Usually, it is 20% of the fund's profit.

31. Catchup

A clause that allows the general partner to take for a limited period of time, a greater share of the carried interest that would normally be allowed.

32. Certified Investor

A term to refer to sophisticated investors. Also called accredited investor.

33. Claw-Back Provision

Claw-back provision in a private equity investment requires the general partner to return any excess distributions of carried interest, if such distributions exceed the share of profits agreed upon by the LPs and GPs. This is known as general partner claw-back. In addition, another common term of private equity partnership agreement is limited partner claw-back, which is intended to protect the general partner against any future claims, should the GP become the subject of a lawsuit. Claw-backs are calculated when a fund is liquidated.

34. Closing

With respect to private equity funds, a "closing" means the time when investors sign the limited partnership agreement and legally commit to provide capital to the fund. There can be one closing or a series of closings. In the case of a series of closings the first closing is known as the "initial closing" and the final closing is known as the "final closing".

35. Collateralized Debt Obligation (CDO)

A collateralized debt obligation (CDO) is a security backed by a pool of debt instruments, such as corporate bonds and corporate loans.

36. Collateralized Loan Obligation (CLO)

A CLO is a security backed by a pool of loans made to corporations by commercial banks.

37. Co-Investment

When the LP invests directly into a portfolio company alongside the private equity fund, it is called co-investment. Usually, co-investment is done through a special purpose vehicle (SPV) established by the GP.

38. Committed Capital

The committed capital in a private equity fund is the total of all individual investment commitments made by the limited partners.

39. Crowdfunding

Crowdfunding is a method of raising small amounts of money from a large number of people in a short period of time to finance a project.

40. Deal Flow

Deal flow refers to the pipeline of investment opportunities available to an investor.

41. Dilution

When a company issues a new round of financing and the existing investors don't participate in the round, there will be a reduction in the percentage ownership of existing investors in the company. This is known as ownership dilution.

42. Discounted Cash Flow (DCF)

Discounted Cash Flow (DCF) valuation is a valuation method to determine the value of a company by projecting its future cashflows and then discounting such cashflows to present value.

43. Distribution

Distribution refers to the distribution of cash or stock to an investor (LP) from the fund.

44. Dividends

Dividends are distributions of profit made by a company in cash or stock to its stockholders.

45. Dividend Capitalization

When a private equity firm refinances debt and uses the funds from such refinancing to pay a special dividend to shareholders, it is known as dividend capitalization.

46. Distribution Waterfall

A distribution waterfall is a method to allocate investment returns among the participants of a pooled investment. In other words the distribution waterfall defines the order in which distributions are allocated to limited and general partners.

47. Dry- Closing

Dry-closing is when a fund closes on the investor commitments to the fund, so the LPs are contractually bound to provide their capital commitments, but the GP does not make an initial capital call for a period of time. There is no fee charged for such period.

48. Due Diligence

Due diligence is the process of evaluating and investigating an investment opportunity for taking an investment decision.

49. Early-stage

Early- stage means a venture capital company has been founded and is in the early stage of developing its technology/products. An early-stage financing means the financing in an early –stage company.

50. Earnings Before Interest, Taxes, Depreciation and Amortization (EBITDA)

EBITDA is a measure to value buyout valuation of a company. A multiple of EBITDA is used to find the sale price of a company.

51. Enterprise Value (EV)

Enterprise value is a measure of a company's total value. It is a fundamental method used in business valuation. It is a sum of claims by all claimants: secured and unsecured creditors and preferred and common shareholders.

52. ESG

ESG stands for Environmental, Social, and Governance framework, that is becoming an important part of the investment process.

For investment professionals a key motivation in the practice of considering environmental, social and governance issues as part of financial analysis is to get a fuller understanding of the investee companies.

53. European Private Equity & Venture Capital Association (EVCA)

EVCA, European private equity & venture capital association represents the private equity community across Europe, including venture capital and infrastructure industry. It is now known as 'Invest Europe'. Invest Europe issues guidelines for the industry and acts as the guardian of the industry.

54. Exit

An "exit" in private equity fund is the act of realising an investment. There are mainly three types of exit strategy: (1) by a trade sale, (2) through an IPO, and (3) secondary buy-out sale (third party sale).

55. Family Office

Family office refers to an entity established by a wealthy family to manage the assets and investments of the family. More and more family offices are set up these days to manage wealth of high net-worth individuals.

56. Final Return

The final return is the return to LPs after all distributions are made and the fund is liquidated.

57. Financing Round

Refers to the process of raising capital in a structured manner by a private equity firm

58. Follow-on-investment

A follow-on-investment in a private equity refers to the additional investment made by an investor in a subsequent financing after his initial investment.

59. Fund-of-Funds

A fund-of-funds is an investment vehicle for the purpose of investing in a portfolio of funds.

60. General Partner (GP)

In the context of a private equity, a general partner is the private equity firm that manages a private equity fund.

61. General Partner Capital Commitment

The amount of capital committed by a general partner in a private equity fund is known as the general partner capital commitment.

62. General Partner Catch-up (GP Catch-up)

A provision in the private equity partnership agreement that allows the GP to get a greater share of the carried interest until the GP has "caught up" with the LPs in the carry structure. Sometimes there is a hurdle rate (preferred return to the LPs) that the GP has to achieve before getting the carried interest. Once the hurdle rate is achieved, the GP receives all of the carry until it is caught up with the carry provisions.

63. GP Claw-back

This is a provision concerning the carried interest requiring the GP to reimburse the fund for the carry received in excess of the provision.

64. Gross Return

Gross return is the total return a fund receives from its investments, before deducting management fee, expenses, and carried interest.

65. Holding Period

Holding period refers to the time period for which an investor holds the investment. Holding period is a deciding factor for calculating the tax liability of the investor.

66. Hurdle Rate

A hurdle rate is the minimum rate of return on an investment required by the manager or investor. Hurdle rate explains the appropriate compensation for the level of risk present in an investment. Riskier investments demand higher hurdle rates than those with less risk.

67. Illiquid Investment

An investment that is not easily saleable An investment in a private equity fund is generally illiquid unlike publicly-traded stocks.

68. Illiquidity Premium

The incremental return an investor demands for investing in an illiquid investment is defined as the illiquidity premium. The required rate of return for an investment in private equity has mainly two components: Illiquidity premium and risk premium.

69. Incubator Firm

An incubator firm is an organization that helps early-stage companies to sail through different developmental stages until the companies have sufficient resources to function on their own. An incubator firm provides start-up companies with low-cost office spaces, resources, and advice.

70. Indian Venture and Alternative capital Association (IVCA)

Indian Venture and Alternative Capital Association (IVCA) is India's apex body representing the interests of Private Equity/Venture Capital industry, Real estate, Infrastructure and Credit funds, Limited Partners, Family offices and Corporate VCs. In the US, the relevant body is National Venture Capital Association (NVCA).

71. Institutional Investors

Institutional investors include sovereign wealth funds (SWF), pension funds, insurance companies, foundations and endowments.

72. Internal Rate of Return (IRR)

IRR is mainly used in private equity investments. It is the annualized rate of return from a series of cash-flows relating to a fund. IRR can be gross or net. Gross IRR is the rate of return without taking into consideration management fees, carried interest and fund expenses. Net IRR is the net return an investor receives after considering management fees, carried interest and fund expenses. Net IRR is what matters to the investor while analyzing an investment opportunity.

73. J Curve

J curve in a private equity or venture capital means the return curve for the investments. It is a graphical representation of the fact that in private equity or venture capital, things get worse before they get better.

74. Key Person

A key person (or key man) is a senior member of the general partner, responsible for managing a fund.

75. Leveraged Buyout (LBO)

Leveraged buyout means purchasing a company using significant amount of debt. The buyer uses the assets of the purchased company as collateral for the debt and pays off the debt using future cash-flows from the company.

76. Limited Partner (LP)

Limited partner in a private equity fund is the investor in the fund. The General partner is the manager of the fund.

77. Limited Partnership

The legal structure used to organize a private equity fund is called the limited partnership.

78. Limited Partnership Agreement (LPA)

A limited partnership agreement is the agreement between the limited partners and general partners of a fund, which sets forth the key terms of the fund, such as management fees, expenses, and carried interest.

79. Liquidation

Liquidation of a private equity fund is the winding process of the fund.

80. Liquidity Event

Liquidity event of a private equity fund is an event by which the investor exits his investment through a sale for cash or through an IPO.

81. Lock-up Period

In an IPO, the initial investors are required to wait for certain period before they can sell their shares in the public market.

Such a restriction is imposed to reduce the volatility and price impact caused by a flood of sale orders.

82. Limited Partner Claw-back

This is a common provision in a limited partnership agreement. In case there is no sufficient funds for a fund to pay a claim, the general partner can require the limited partners to pay back part of the profit received by the LP to pay the claim.

83. Management Buyout (MBO)

Management buyout is a leveraged buyout where the management of a company leads the buyout process.

84. Management Fee

The fee charged by the general partner for running the day to day operation of a fund. Usually, it is 2% of the committed capital each year during the investment period.

85. Merger

Merger is the process by which two companies voluntarily combine to form one entity.

86. Mezzanine Debt (Mezzanine Financing)

Mezzanine debt or mezzanine financing is a form of debt financing in a leveraged buyout. Mezzanine debt is junior to all senior debt, but senior to all equity.

87. Minimum Commitment

Most private equity funds have a minimum amount requirement for an investor to come in as a limited partner. Usually, it is $5 million to $10 million for a US private equity fund.

88. National Venture Capital Association (NVCA)

The National Venture Capital Association (NVCA) is an organization that represents US venture capital community. The NVCA represents the venture industry in public policy debates in America and promotes high professional standards. In India IVCA is the relevant body.

89. Operating Partner

Operating partner of a private equity is a person with high experience and expertise, who assists in the management of the firm's operations.

90. Organizational Expense

The expenses for organising and marketing a private equity fund.

91. Paid –In-Capital

The capital contributed by a limited partner from his committed capital is known as paid-in-capital.

92. Pari Passu

Pari passu is a Latin phrase meaning "equal footing". In finance this means that all parties to a financial contract are treated the same.

93. Payment – In – Kind (PIK)

When a company pays stock of the company as dividend instead of cash dividend, it is called payment-in-kind (PIK).

94. Private Equity Fund

A private equity fund is a pooled investment vehicle which pools together money and uses that money to make investments on behalf of the fund. The investments are long-term that takes time to sell and hence the investment time horizon is typically 10 or more years. A private equity fund has limited partners (LP) and general partners (GP). Limited Partners typically own 99% of shares in a fund and have limited liability. General Partners own 1% of shares and have full liability. GP is responsible for executing and operating the investment.

95. Private Equity Firms (Managers)

Private equity managers are managers of private equity funds, who earn money by charging management fees and performance fees from investors in a fund. The primary source of revenue for private equity firms is management fees. In addition they receive performance fees. Typically management fee is 2% of the funds under management and performance fee is 20% of the profits generated from the sale of a company.

96. Pipeline Deals

In a private equity, this refers to the deal flow the private equity has.

97. Placement Agent

A placement agent, usually an investment bank, that helps the funds raise capital

98. Platform Company

A company acquired by a private equity firm to serve as a platform for further acquisitions and growth.

99. Portfolio Company

A company in which a private equity fund has made an investment is known as a portfolio company.

100. Pre-Emptive Right

Pre-emptive right, otherwise called subscription right, is the right of existing shareholders to acquire new shares issued by a company in a right issue.

101. Preferred Return

A provision in a private equity agreement which provides the limited partners a threshold return before the general partner is entitled to receive any carried interest.

102. Private Equity

Private equity refers to an equity investment in a privately – held firm.

103. Private Placement Memorandum (PPM)

PPM is the marketing document summarizing the terms of a private placement to investors. This is a key document for fund raising as it sets out the investment philosophy of the fund, the investment objective, the management fee and other terms and conditions.

104. Pro Rata

Pro rata refers to the right of an investor in a venture capital to participate in a future financing round so that the investor maintains his ownership share in the company.

105. Public-to-Private (P2P)

This refers to a publicly quoted company being taken into private ownership.

106. Recapitalization

A recapitalization means a restructuring of a company's capital structure in terms of equity and debt.

107. Return on Investment (ROI)

It is the percentage return on an investment.

108. Revolving Credit

Revolving credit facility refers to an arrangement that allows companies to borrow up to their credit limit without having to apply each time they need cash. As they repay the money borrowed, the money is again available to be borrowed again.

109. Secured Debt

The debt of a company secured by the specific assets of the company is known as secured debt. In case the company defaults on the debt, the lender has the right to seize those specific assets.

110. Senior Debt

Senior debt ranks above all other types of debt such as subordinated debt and unsecured debt.

111. Special Purpose Vehicle (SPV)

A Special purpose vehicle is a separate legal entity created by an organization for a specific objective. SPV will have its own assets and liabilities. As it is a separate legal entity, if the parent company goes bankrupt, the special purpose vehicle can carry on.

112. Stock Option

When a company gives its employees a benefit by way of " stock option" which gives the employee a right (but not the obligation) to buy the shares of the company at a certain price (strike price) for a certain period of time (usually 10 years), with certain conditions, it is called a 'stock option'.

113. Strategic Investor

A "strategic investor" is a big company that makes a substantial investment in a startup company for deriving some benefits out of the growth of the startup company or to acquire the company ultimately.

114. Term of a Fund

The term of a fund as stated in the limited partnership agreement, usually 10 years. There can be further extensions of 1-2 years at the discretion of the general partner.

115. Term Sheet

Term sheet is a document that lists the primary terms of a fund.

116. Trade Sale

Trade sale occurs when a portfolio company in a private equity fund is sold to an operating company in the same or similar industry.

117. Venture Capital (VC)

Venture capital is a form of private equity financing that is provided by venture capital firms to startup, early stage and emerging companies that are deemed to have high potential for growth.

118. Vintage Year

The year in which a fund starts is known as the "vintage year'. Another definition is that the "vintage year" is the year in which a fund makes its first investment.

119. Write - Down

When the carrying value of an investment is reduced, but not to zero, it is known as a "write-down".

120. Write-Off

When the carrying value of an investment is reduced to zero, it is known as a "write-off".

121. Write-Up

When the carrying value of an investment is increased, it is known as a "write-up".

CHAPTER 10

Venture Capital

VENURE CAPITAL (VC)

Venture Capital is defined as money, technical, or managerial expertise provided by investors to startup firms which have long-term growth potential. The venture capital industry has four main players: entrepreneurs who need funding; investors who want high returns; investment bankers who need companies to sell; and the venture capitalists who make money for themselves. Venture capital is contributed generally by high net-worth investors, investment banks, and any other financial institutions. However venture capital funding is not limited to money alone, but also includes technical or managerial expertise. While investments of this type carry a greater risk, the potential for relatively higher return makes such investments attractive.

While the venture capital industry in the U.S has a long track record, venture capital in India has a short history. The venture capital industry in India evolved in the late 1980s with the Government of India legalizing venture capital operation in 1988. Since then, the industry has recorded tremendous growth as well as several regulatory reviews and innovations. In 1988, ICICI emerged as the first capital provider with UTI. There are more than 800 venture capital firms in India currently.

1. ARPU

Average Revenue Per User

2. AOV

Average Order Value

3. Early Stage Financing

Early Stage is the first round in which a VC firm provides capital. This stage of financing has the highest level of risk as the visibility of the project is least. This is also known as A-round financing.

4. Exit Stage

A VC firm also creates value through exit. The exit can happen through three primary avenues: IPO, Acquisition by a financial buyer, and Acquisition by a trade buyer.

5. Mid Stage Financing

If the initial VC firm or another investor provides additional capital as needed by the company, this is known as B-round financing or mid stage financing.

6. Late Stage Financing

Late stage financing occurs after A-round and B-round financing, when a company has produced sales, revenue, profits and there is visibility into an exit.

7. Startup and Seed Stage

The startup and seed stage are primarily concerned with financing the initial concept or product introduced by the founder.

8. Venture Lending

Venture Lending is defined as a debt offered either by a bank or a non-bank to any company that is still reliant on VC support.

(More VC jargons can be found in the chapter under Private equity).

CHAPTER 11

Real Estate

Real Estate

Real estate is a significant part of the Alternative asset class. Real estate offers investors long-term stable income, some protection from inflation, capital gain and generally low correlation with stocks and bonds. High-quality and well-managed properties with low leverage are expected to generate higher returns than high-grade debt (of course with higher risk) and lower returns and lower risk than equity. Real estate investments are less liquid than traditional asset classes. However real estate investment is an effective means of diversification in a balanced investment portfolio. Real estate is mainly of two types: residential and commercial. Residential real estate constitutes the largest portion of the real estate market, which is mostly owner occupied. Then there are commercial properties which include office buildings, shopping centers, and warehouses. Pension funds, sovereign wealth funds, insurance companies, and high net-worth individuals are the largest investors in real estate. Real estate investments have four basic forms: Private equity (direct ownership), publicly traded equity (indirect ownership), private debt (mortgage lending), and publicly traded debt (securitized mortgages). A student of finance or an investor has to be familiar with various terminologies used in the real estate phase to better understand this asset class.

1. As-is

A property marketed "As is" condition means the seller is unwilling to perform most of the repairs. This type of property is usually priced lower than the market price.

2. Backup Offer

When a buyer is interested in purchasing a property which is already under a contract with someone else, that buyer has an opportunity to submit a "backup offer", in case the first transaction doesn't go through.

3. Blind Offer

When a buyer makes an offer for a property he hasn't seen, that offer is called a "blind offer".

4. Break-even Ratio (BER)

Break-even = (Operating Expenses + Debt Service) /Gross Operating Income

5. Built-up Area

Built-up area is the area that comes after adding carpet area and wall area (thickness of the walls). In other words, it is the area of an apartment, measured from the external perimeter of the wall surface. As per RERA, the built-up area also consists of other areas mandated by the authorities, such as dry balcony, flower beds, etc. In apartments in India, nearly 30% of the entire area of the apartment is used for creating the inner walls and the balconies. Hence if the built-up area of the apartment is 1,000 Sq.ft, one can assume that the carpet area is 700 sq.ft.(Please refer to RERA rules for further information).

6. Buyer's Agent

A buyer's agent is a licensed real estate professional whose job is to locate a suitable property for the buyer, by undertaking all negotiations on behalf of that buyer. An agent's commission is typically 2-3% of the contract price.

7. Ratio (Cap Rate)

Cap Rate = Net Operating Income / Total Cost of Property Price

8. Carpet Area

As the name indicates, carpet area of an apartment is the area you could cover with carpet. According to RERA, Carpet area is the net usable area of an apartment, excluding the area covered by the external walls, areas under service shafts, exclusive balcony or verandah area, and exclusive open terrace area, but includes the area covered by the internal partition walls of the apartment. As per RERA, builders have to sell their properties based on RERA carpet area.

9. Cash Flow

Cashflow is the net operating income of a property minus the debt service payments.

10. Completion Certificate

A completion certificate is a document issued by the competent authority after inspection of the real estate project, stating that the construction has been made as per approved building plan and it meets all standards set by the competent authority.

11. Conventional Sale

A conventional sale is when the property is free of any mortgage.

12. Covenants, Conditions & Restrictions (CC&Rs)

These are the rules and regulations placed on a real property by a residential association, a developer, or a builder.

13. Closing

Closing means a home sale is considered final. This includes signing all documents, and conveying all moneys.

14. Closing Costs

Closing costs are fees charged by a lender, title company, attorney, real estate agents, tax authorities, and other closing related companies.

15. CREDAI

The Confederation of Real Estate Developers' Association of India (CREDAI) is an association of real estate developers and builders with a view to safeguarding the interests of consumers and promoting fair trade in the real estate market. CREDAI is the apex body for the private real estate in India. CREDAI, established in 1999, aims to make the real estate industry organized and progressive by working closely with the all stakeholders, consumers, policymakers, finance companies and professionals.

16. Days On Market (DOM)

DOM is defined as the number of days from the date on which a property is listed for sale to the date when the seller has signed a contract for the sale of the property.

17. Debt-to-Income ratio (DTI)

DTI is a ratio used by mortgage lenders which is calculated by the total debt expenses, plus monthly housing payment, divided by the gross monthly income.

18. Dry Lease

Dry lease refers to hiring aircraft from another airline without a crew.

19. Due Diligence

Due diligence is the process of examining a property,by hiring experts to inspect the property, perform tests, etc so that the buyer decides to proceed.

20. Earnest Money Deposit (EMD)

An earnest money deposit (EMD) is the initial funds a buyer is asked to put down once a seller accepts the buyer's offer.

21. Equity

This refers to the investment a homeowner has in his home. It is calculated by taking the market value of the home and subtracting any mortgages or liens against the property.

22. Fixed Rate Mortgage

With fixed rate mortgage, the interest rate stays the same for the duration of the loan.

23. Rental Yield

Annual rent from a property divided by the total property cost multiplied by 100.

24. Hard Money Loan

A way to borrow money based on the property and not considering the credit score

25. Infrastructure Investment Trust (InvITS)

Infrastructure Investment Trusts (InvITS) are investment instruments designed to promote infrastructure investments in India by providing individual investors a platform for investing in real estate. It is regulated by SEBI and broadly, it works like a mutual fund. The units of InvITS are listed on stock exchanges in India. Thus typically, this trust pools money from investors for investing in income generating properties and distribute the income generated as dividend income. The structure and operation of both REITs and InvITS are similar, but there are some differences.

26. Land Lease

Traditionally, when you purchase a home, you own the home and the land on which the home is built. However there are some circumstances that involve a land lease, which means you own the home while paying rent to the landowner for the land.

27. Loan to Value Ratio

Loan to Value = Loan Amount / Value of the Property

28. Location

Location is a key factor in valuing real estate. Location takes into consideration the accessibility (roads, buses, railway stations, etc), amenities in the neighbourhood such as schools, hospitals, worship centers, police and fire stations, shopping malls, petrol stations, etc.

29. Net Operating Income (NOI)

Gross income of a property minus expenses

30. Occupancy Certificate

The certificate issued by a local authority certifying that the building is fit for occupation, and has been constructed as per approved plan and is in compliance with local laws.

31. Preliminary Report

A preliminary report reveals any issues with the title that need to be dealt with by the seller in order to get a clear title. This report is needed for a title insurance company to issue a title insurance policy.

32. Probate Sale

A probate sale happens when a homeowner dies without writing a will or leaving a property to someone. In the U.S., a probate court would authorize an estate attorney or other representative, to hire a real estate agent to sell the home.

33. Proof of Funds

When you make an offer for a home, sellers will require you to submit proof of funds, either cash or a mortgage.

34. Purchase and Sale Agreement (PSA)

A written contract between the buyer and seller of a property, which outlines the terms of the transaction

35. Realtors

A realtor in the U.S is a member of the National Association of Realtors (NAR). An actively licensed real estate agent and realtor are often used interchangeably.

36. Real Estate Investment Trusts (REITs)

A real estate investment trust (REIT) is a company that owns, operates or finances income-generating real estate. REITs pool the capital of many investors, like mutual funds. This makes it possible for individual investors to participate in real estate investments and earn dividends without having to own or manage properties themselves. REITs generate a steady income for investors but offer limited opportunities for capital appreciation. Most REITs in the U.S are publicly traded like stocks, making them highly liquid. REITs mainly invest in apartments, warehouses, office buildings, retail centers, medical facilities and hotels. In India the concept of REIT was born recently, but have gained significant popularity. There are some good performing REITs in India.

37. Real Estate Regulatory Authority (RERA)

Real Estate Regulatory Act 2016 is an act of the Indian Parliament that intends to protect the interests of home buyers and to increase the transparency in the real estate sector in India. The Act has established Real Estate Regulatory Authority (RERA) in each state for the regulation of the real estate sector.

38. Rent-back or Lease-back

Rent-back (Lease back) is an arrangement whereby the buyer of a home allows the seller to continue to stay in the home for an agreed period, based on terms which are negotiated prior to the closing.

39. Rental Bond

A rental bond is a three-way agreement between the landlord, the tenant, and the surety provider for protecting the landlord from losses arising out from a tenant's default. The rental bond company called the surety provider underwrites the tenant and issues a bond after it has been satisfied with the credibility of the tenant. If the tenant defaults, the rental bond pays the landlord the amount of loss upto the amount of indemnity covered in the bond. Losses more than the indemnity are collected by the bond from the defaulting tenant.

40. Rent Ratio

Rent Ratio = Monthly Rent / Cost of the property

41. Return on Investment (ROI)

ROI = (Cashflow + Principal Payment) / Investment

42. Seller Disclosure

A seller's disclosure is a disclosure about the property, which could affect a buyer's decision to purchase the property.

43. Short Sale

Short sale of a property happens when the property is sold for less than the debt amount secured by the property. Short sales will require the approval of the lender as the sale proceeds will be less than amount owed. Typically a short sale will be a long process.

44. Super Built-up Area

Super built-up area is the area calculated by adding the built-up area and common area that includes the corridor, lift and lift lobby, etc. In some cases, builders even add amenities such as a pool, garden or club house in the common area. A builder charges a buyer on the basis of super built-up area. It is also called saleable area. However, RERA rules state that builders have to sell apartments based on RERA carpet area. (Please refer to RERA rules for clarification).

45. Tenancy In Common (TIC)

TIC is a type of joint ownership of a property, whether a single family property or a commercial building, where the tenants in common all own the property, but in different ratios.

46. Title Search

A title search means an examination of the public records for the history of the home, including prior sales and purchases, and tax and other type of liens.

47. Trust Sale

A trust sale means that the home is being sold by a trustee of a living trust. This is because the original owner has passed away, or has placed the home in a living trust.

48. Wet Lease

Wet lease means hiring aircrafts by an airline from another airline for operations without buying them. Sometimes wet lease includes the crew and fuel.

CHAPTER 12

Mortgage Securities

1. Adjustable-Rate Mortgage (ARM)

A mortgage loan with an interest rate that is periodically adjusted based on an index reflecting the cost to the lender for borrowing in the credit markets. In a falling interest rate environment, adjustable - rate mortgage is recommended.

2. Aggregator

An entity that purchases mortgage loans from financial institutions and securitizes them into mortgage-backed securities which are then sold to investors in the secondary mortgage market

3. Amortization

The gradual reduction in the principal amount owed on a mortgage debt. During the early years of the loan, most of each payment is applied towards the interest owed. During the final years of the loan, payment amounts are applied exclusively to the remaining principal.

4. Amortization Table or Schedule

A timetable or schedule that gives you a breakdown of your monthly payments into principal and interest. This table shows you the amount of principal you will be repaying during your mortgage term.

5. Time

The time required to pay off the loan, expressed in months

6. Annual Adjustment Cap

A limit on how much the variable interest on a loan can increase or decrease each year

7. Annual Percentage Rate (APR)

The annual cost of a loan, expressed as a percentage. However it can include other charges or fees for insurance, and closing costs.

8. Appraiser

A person whose job is to assess the monetary value of an asset. For obtaining a mortgage, it is necessary to obtain an appraised value of the property from an appraiser.

9. Appraised Value

An appraised value is the assessed value of a property in the opinion of a qualified appraiser. It is a pre-qualification for obtaining a mortgage loan.

10. Appreciation

An increase in the value of a property over time. The key factors contributing to the appreciation of a property are its location, market value of comparable properties in that locality, age of the property, prevailing demand and supply situation and interest rate environment. Appreciation of a property increases its equity, which in turn increases the amount one can borrow for a home equity line of credit.

11. Approved Term

The number of months that will take to pay off a mortgage loan. The term includes the payment amount, repayment schedule, and the total interest to be paid over the life of the loan.

12. Approved Lender

Lenders that meet the requirements established by regulatory authorities for origination, underwriting, purchasing, holding, servicing, or selling mortgages. The lender has to pass an eligibility requirement which includes net worth threshold, financial statements, and a quality control programme.

13. Approved Seller

An institution approved to sell mortgages. The institution has to satisfy certain eligibility requirements including a net worth threshold, financial statements and a quality control programme.

14. Assessed Value

The value of a property established by an assessor. The assessed value is used to determine property taxes.

15. Balloon Loan

A loan that involves a lower than usual monthly payments for an initial period of time followed by a larger than usual payment at the end of the loan repayment period. Be aware that interest payments will be higher in such loans.

16. Base Rate

The definition of base rate varies from country to country. Broadly a base rate is the interest rate that a central bank –such as Federal Reserve or Bank of England will charge commercial banks for loans.

A base rate is used as a benchmark for pricing variable-rate loans, auto loans and credit cards. In India base rate is the minimum rate set by the Reserve Bank of India below which banks are not allowed to lend to its customers.

17. Basis Point

One one-hundredth of one percent (1/100 or 0.01)

18. Broker

A third party who negotiates a contract between parties, but does not lend the money.

19. Broker Fees

Fees charged by a real estate broker for providing assistance in a real estate transaction

20. Closing

The time and place, at which all documents for a loan are signed, dated, and notarized.

21. Closing costs

Fees incurred by the borrower and/or seller for costs associated with the closing transaction

22. Collateral

An asset, such as a car or a home, used for securing the payment of a loan. If the loan is not repaid, the borrower stands to lose the asset.

23. Collaterized Mortgage Obligation (CMO)

A Collaterized Mortgage Obligation (CMO) is a type of mortgage-backed security that contains a pool of mortgages bundled together and sold as an investment. Since the pool has mortgages with different maturities and levels of risk, CMOs receive cashflows as borrowers repay the mortgages that act as collateral. In turn, CMOs distribute principal and interest payments to their investors based on predetermined rules and agreements.

24. Conventional Loan

A mortgage that is not insured or guaranteed by a Federal agency. In the U.S the federal agencies include Federal Housing Administration, U.S Department of Housing and Urban Development, the U.S Department of Veterans Affairs, U.S Department of Agriculture and the Department of Indian Affairs. In India the RBI and its supporting organizations are entrusted by the Government with implementing framework and rules for mortgage business.

25. Correspondent Lender

A lending institution that originates and funds loans in its own name and then sells them to another lender or investor

26. Credit Score

A number that determines the quality of an individual's credit. The number helps to predict the likelihood that a borrower will repay a credit obligation, such as a mortgage loan.

27. Deed

A document that legally transfers ownership of real estate from the seller to the buyer and delivered to the buyer at closing

28. Default

Failure to make mortgage payments on time or to meet other terms of a loan.

29. Down Payment

A payment made in cash at the onset of taking a mortgage loan. Typically home owners pay down payments that equal 5-25 per cent of the total value of a home in the U.S.The minimum down payment for home loan in India is set at 20%. The RBI has directed banks and NBFCs to grant only 80% of the property value as loan and the rest 20% has to be arranged by the borrower. This 20% is the down payment in this case.

30. Earnest Money

A deposit made toward a down payment as a sign of good faith, which is typically made when a purchase agreement is signed. The earnest money deposit is also known as a token money, binder, front money, security deposit, or good- faith deposit.

31. Encumbrance

Any lien or liability attached to a property that affects or limits the title to that property

32. Equated Monthly Installments (EMI)

EMI or an Equated monthly installment is the monthly payment the borrower has to make to the lender as part of the repayment schedule. The EMI accounts for both home loan principal amount and the interest accumulated, which the borrower is liable to pay back in full. A Home Loan EMI calculator facilitates the calculation of an EMI.

33. Escrow

Funds deposited with a third party, to be held until a specific date or a specific condition is met.

34. Fair Market Value

Fair market value of a home is the likely selling price of the home, as determined by a property appraiser.

35. Fannie Mae (FNMA)

The Federal National Mortgage Association (FNMA), commonly known as Fannie Mae, is a United States government-sponsored enterprise and a leading source of mortgage financing in the United States.

36. Federal Housing Administration (FHA)

An agency of the Department of Housing and Urban Development. The FHA provides mortgage insurance for certain residential mortgages.

37. First Mortgage

A mortgage in the first-lien position that has priority over all other liens or claims in the event of a default

38. Fixed - Rate Mortgage

In a fixed-rate mortgage, the interest rate is set when the borrower takes out the mortgage and does not change over the term of the loan. In a rising interest rate environment, fixed-rate mortgage is recommended.

39. Forbearance

The term forbearance refers to the temporary postponement of a loan (mortgage or student loan). Lenders and creditors are willing to grant forbearance as an alternative to foreclosure or default.

40. Foreclosure

A legal procedure in which the property securing a defaulted loan is sold by the lender to meet the repayment of a borrower's loan

41. Forfeiture

Forfeiture means the loss of rights, property, or money, as a result of breaking a legal agreement.

42. Freddie Mac (FHLMC)

Freddie Mac is the officially recognized nickname for the Federal Home Loan Mortgage Corp (FHLMC) in the U.S. It is a government – sponsored enterprise to support home ownership by middle-income Americans.

43. Ginnie Mae (GNMA)

Short for Government National Mortgage Association. GNMA is a U.S. government agency that guarantees timely payments on mortgage-backed securities (MBS). For doing this GNMA works with other governmental agencies to make affordable housing widely available through mortgage loans.

44. Haircut

A haircut is the percentage difference between the market value of an asset and the asset's worth relative to how much a lender will recognise of that value as collateral. It is also called the market maker's spread. For example, if a person needs a $10,000 loan and wants to offer his $10,000 stock portfolio as collateral, the lending bank is more likely to recognise the $10,000 portfolio as worth only $6,000 in collateral. The $4,000 or 40% reduction in the asset's value, for collateral purpose, is called the haircut. In this case, if the stock portfolio declines in value due to market gyrations, the lender may still have enough collateral for the loan given.

45. HUD

An acronym for the U.S. Department of Housing and Urban Development. HUD is a government agency responsible for the implementation and administration of housing and urban development programmes.

46. Insured Mortgage

A mortgage that is protected by an insurer in case of default

47. Loan –to-Value Ratio (LTV)

LTV is the ratio that compares the amount of the mortgage with the appraised value of the property. It is calculated by dividing the loan amount by the value of the property.

48. Manufactured Housing

A structure that has been partially or entirely constructed at another location and moved on to the property on a permanent foundation

49. Master Commitment

A contractual agreement between the purchaser and seller of mortgages, that provides the terms of the sale.

50. Mobile Home

A type of home that is built upon a wheeled chassis and can be transported from place to place

51. Modular Home

A factory built home that is erected on site, with the appearance and characteristics of a site-built residence.

52. Mortgage Insurance

An insurance policy paid for by the borrower with the lender as beneficiary, in which the insurer takes some of the loan – default risk.

53. Mortgage Pool (Pool)

A group of mortgage loans acquired under one or more loan funding commitments, contractual agreements or similar arrangements

54. Multi-Family Residence

A residential property with 2 to 4 individual housing units

55. Negative Amortization

When the monthly payments are less than the interest due on a home loan, the situation is called a negative amortization. The unpaid interest is added to the unpaid balance and the home buyer will owe increasingly more than the original amount of the loan.

56. Origination

The date that the proceeds of a loan are disbursed

57. Payoff

Payment of the outstanding balance of a loan in full

58. PITI

PITI is an acronym for Principal, Interest, Taxes and Insurance, when referring to monthly mortgage charges.

59. Prepayment

An amount paid to reduce the principal balance of a loan before the principal is due

60. Prepayment Risk

A risk that banks can face if they grant homeowners the option to take advantage of lower mortgage interest rates by refinancing their mortgages on more favourable terms, resulting in prepayment of the existing loan. In such situations, the banks face reinvestment risk of investing those funds at lower rates.

61. Prime Rate

The interest rate that banks charge their best customers when lending them money. The Wall Street Journal publishes daily the US Prime Rate, which is based on a survey of the prime rates of the 10 largest banks in the United States. The US Prime Rate serves as a benchmark for the calculation of various interest rate products in US Dollars such as mortgage interest rates, credit card charges, loans by banks, and so on. In India the boards of banks have been empowered to decide the Benchmark Prime Lending Rate (BPLR), as also the spread over BPLR. The prime lending rate in India is the average rate of interest charged on loans by five major banks. Retail Prime Lending Rate (RPLR), is the rate at which housing finance companies (HFCs) lend to their most creditworthy customers. It is the benchmark against which these lenders price their loans to customers. RPLR is derived from the average cost of funds for the HFCs.

62. Rate Lock

A commitment issued by a lender to a borrower guaranteeing a specific interest rate for a specified time. After the expiry of that specified time, you have to negotiate a new rate lock prior to closing your loan.

63. Refinance

Refinance means paying off an existing loan using the proceeds of a new loan, generally using the same property as collateral, in order to take advantage of lower interest rates and lower monthly payments.

64. Representations and Guarantees

The assertions that a seller makes in a purchase and sale agreement about the nature of the loan, which in turn form the basis for due diligence process. This ensures that loan originators comply with the credit terms required by the secondary market entities.

65. Reverse Mortgage

Reverse mortgage is a loan that allows senior citizens to draw on their homes' equity. The loan provides an additional source of income for senior citizens, who have self-acquired homes. It is an alternative to selling or moving out of the house in order to generate a fixed income stream to meet their requirements while they go through their retired lives. Most of the senior citizens have a property in their names; but the same cannot be converted into instant or regular income stream due to its illiquid nature. Through the reverse mortgage they can have the cake and eat it too. The house owner can mortgage his property with a financial institution and the financial institution pays the house owner a regular income and the borrower is not expected to service the loan during his lifetime. While the concept of reverse mortgage has been used in the U.S for a long time, it is a new concept in India. The financial institution has the right to sell the property after the death of the customer and the excess amount will be remitted back to the legal heirs. If the legal heirs clear the loan after the death of the house owner, they can own the house. In the U.S reverse mortgage is of various types: Proprietary, Jumbo, and Single-purpose reverse mortgage.

66. Right of First Refusal

A provision in an agreement that requires the owner of a property to give another party the first opportunity to purchase or lease the property before the owner offers it for sale or lease to others.

67. Sanction Letter

The home loan sanction letter is a formal letter that confirms the loan approval. It is the legal proof of the home loan eligibility and approval.

68. Secondary Mortgage Market

Market in which previously issued mortgages and mortgage-backed securities are traded among lenders and investors

69. Subprime Mortgage

Subprime mortgage is a loan given to individuals who do not qualify for prime-rate loans. The interest rate on this loan is higher than that offered for prime-rate loans. These mortgages allow less-worthy borrowers to own a house but at much higher interest rates. It may be remembered that the main contributor to the global financial crisis of 2007-2008 was the subprime mortgage market. Subprime mortgages are now making a comeback as nonprime mortgages.

70. Subordinate Financing

Any mortgage or other lien that has priority lower than that of the first mortgage.In the case of a foreclosure the subordinate loan has a claim only after the first mortgage is paid.

71. Tenor

Tenor is the repayment timeline of a home loan specified by the lender. The borrower has to pay off the interest and principal, within the allocated time. The usual tenor is 30 years in India.

72. Title Company

An agency that will investigate a property's title for discrepancies or undisclosed liens

73. Upfront Costs

The costs you must pay when applying for a loan. Typically this includes loan application fees.

74. VA Loan

A mortgage that is guaranteed by the U.S Department of Veterans Affairs (VA) for qualified veterans of U.S military forces.

75. Variable Rate

An interest rate that fluctuates or changes periodically, in relation to an index such as the prime rate

CHAPTER 13

Hedge Funds

HEDGE FUNDS

Hedge funds form an important part of the Alternative Investments asset class. A hedge fund is a pooled investment fund that can invest in a wide variety of products, including derivatives, foreign exchange, and publicly traded securities. Hedge fund is able to make extensive use of more complex trading, portfolio construction, and risk management techniques such as short selling, leverage and use of derivatives to earn a higher rate of return. In other words, a hedge fund is a limited partnership of private investors whose money is managed by professional fund managers who use a wide range of investment strategies to earn above average returns. Although hedge funds have existed for many decades, they have become increasingly popular in recent years. It is estimated that hedge fund assets total nearly $5 trillion as of 2023. The return of hedge funds depends very much on manager skill. Investment in hedge funds is most suited to sophisticated investors and/or institutional investors. Hedge funds are not suitable for retail investors, who lack expertise to analyse the nature and risks of hedge funds. Hedge fund investors typically include high net worth individuals, family endowments, pension funds, insurance companies, and banks. Hedge funds are relatively less regulated relative to traditional mutual funds, as a result of which hedge fund managers can take long/short positions in almost all financial instruments and use extremely high levels of leverage. Alfred W. Jones, an Australian investor, may be regarded as the **"father of hedge fund industry",** as he is believed to have started the first hedge in 1949, pursuing a strategy of buying stocks and hedging those positions with short sales. While the hedge fund industry is quite advanced in the U.S and some world markets, it has a short history in India. Having said that, the median Indian hedge fund has outperformed the average global hedge fund during the corona pandemic period of 2020-2021 period as per Eureka Indian Hedge Fund Index data.

1. Accredited Investor

An investor who has a net worth of $1 million in invested assets

2. Activist Investor

An activist investor, typically a specialised hedge fund, buys a significant minority stake in a publicly traded company in order to change the way, it is run. An activist investor attempts to pressure its management into making changes or replacing its management.

3. Alpha

The return of a portfolio over and above that of an appropriate benchmark

4. Attribution

The process of attributing returns to their sources, such as stock selection, industry selection, under-weighting/over-weighting and so on

6. Beta

Beta is a measure of systematic non-diversifiable risk. The purpose of the measure is to quantify how much systematic risk is being taken by the fund manager.

7. Convertible Bond Arbitrage

Convertible bond arbitrage is an investment strategy of taking simultaneous long and short positions in a convertible bond and its underlying stock.

8. Correlation

Measure of how strategy returns move with one another.

9. Delta Hedge

How the price of an option responds to the movement in the price of the underlying stock

10. Directional Exposure

The amount of risk an un-hedged position faces in the market, as compared to the net exposure of positions involving long and short hedged relationship.

11. Drawdown

The percentage loss from a fund's highest value to its lowest, over a given time frame. The ratio is looked at as a measure of potential risk.

12. Equity Market Neutral

An investment strategy where the manager attempts to take advantage of differences in stock prices by being long and short an equal amount of closely related stocks within the same sector, industry, and country.

13. Fund of Funds (FOF)

A fund of funds (FOF) is a pooled fund that invests in other hedge funds. It is also known as multi-manager investment.

14. Hedging

Hedging is a risk management strategy used to offset the losses in an investment by taking an opposite position in a related asset.

15. Hedge Ratio

The hedge ratio is a comparison of the value of a position protected by the use of a hedge with the size of the total position.

16. High Water Marks

This is a clause to prevent a manager from receiving duplicate performance compensation following period of volatility. Most funds require investors to recoup past losses before the fund manager is entitled for additional performance compensation. In order to address this situation, a high water mark is stipulated. For example, suppose a fund starts with a capital of $100 million. In the first year the fund realizes a return of 20%, and the value increases to $120 million. This peak value is the High water mark. In the next year if the value of the fund is less than $120 million, the manager does not get any performance fees.

17. Hurdle Rate

Some funds require the investment manager to achieve a certain level of return, before the manager is entitled to receive performance compensation. This means that the manager receives compensation that exceeds the hurdle rate.

18. Leverage

Leverage shows the amount of borrowing used in a fund. Leverage can magnify the performance if the borrowing is used to make good investments. However it can also magnify the loss if the leverage is used to make bad investments.

19. Liquidity

Liquidity refers to the periods (monthly, quarterly, yearly) when investors can redeem their investments and get back their money. Be aware that the investment performance can vary from the time of serving redemption notice to the actual redemption.

20. Lock-up Period

The time period an investor must remain invested before he can redeem his investment.

21. Long/Short Equity

Long/Short equity is a popular hedge fund strategy of buying stocks which are underpriced and selling stocks which are overpriced.

22. Management Fees

Management fees for hedge fund typically ranges from 1% to 2% annually. Management fee is intended to cover manager salaries and general overhead.

23. Net Market Exposure

The percentage of a portfolio exposed to the market fluctuation, taking both long positions and short positions into consideration

24. Neutral Hedge

A hedge that is expected to yield a dollar-neutral result of the combined position

25. Pairs Trading

A long/short trading strategy where one stock is bought and a similar stock is sold, often within the same industry

26. Performance Fees

The hedge fund manager's share in the fund's profits. The performance fee is a percentage allocation of the increase in the value of the fund's assets, and is usually around 20%.

27. Portfolio Simulation

Testing an investment strategy by simulating it with a database and analytic software

28. Qualified Investor

An investor holding at least $5 million in investments

29. Quant Funds

A Quant Fund is an investment fund (Hedge Fund) that uses quantitative investment management instead of fundamental analysis. Managers use algorithms and computer models to select investments.

30. Risk Arbitrage

Refers to a strategy of taking a long position in the stock of a target company, and short position in the stock of the acquiring company

31. R-Squared

It is a measure of what portion of a portfolio's performance can be explained by the performance of a market index

32. Run on a Fund

Refers to growing amount of redemption request in a hedge fund.

33. Short Interest Rebate

When you borrow a stock and sell it short, the sale proceeds are credited to your account. The interest on that cash is called short rebate.

34. Short Sale

Short sale refers to the practice of borrowing a stock on collateral and immediately selling it with a view to buying it back later at a lower price when the market corrects.

35. Standard Deviation

Standard deviation is a measure of the average deviation from an expected result. The higher the deviation, the riskier the investment.

36. Sharpe Ratio

This is a ratio named after William F. Sharpe, the U.S economist. The Sharpe ratio compares the return of an investment with its risk. It is computed by the fund's return over the risk-free rate by the standard deviation of returns.

37. Traditional Investing

Traditional investing, known also as long - only investing, is the strategy of buying undervalued securities with the hope of selling it a higher price to generate profit.

38. Value at Risk (VaR)

Value at risk (VaR) is a statistic that quantifies the extent of possible financial loss in an investment or a portfolio over a given time frame. Risk managers use VaR to measure the level of risk exposure and control it.

CHAPTER 14

Financial Derivatives

Financial Derivatives

Financial derivatives are defined as financial contracts, set between two or more parties, that derive their value from an underlying financial asset, group of assets, or benchmark. Financial derivatives are used to manage financial risks by trading them privately or on an exchange. OTC derivatives constitute the greater proportion of derivatives trade. Financial derivatives are used for a number of purposes including risk management, hedging, arbitrage between markets, and speculation.

Different Types of Derivatives

There are several types of financial derivatives. Following are the examples of some widely used derivatives:

- Forward Contracts

A privately negotiated contract between a buyer and a seller to trade an asset at a future date at a price agreed at the initiation of the contract.

- Futures Contracts

A standardized legal agreement to buy or sell a particular commodity, asset, or security at a predetermined price at a specified time in the future.

- Options Contracts

Options are financial derivatives that give buyers the right, but not the obligation, to buy or sell an underlying asset at an agreed-upon price within a stated period. Call options and put options are the two forms of options. A call option gives the holder the right to buy an asset at an agreed price within a stated period. Put option is the opposite of call option. Put option gives the buyer the right to sell an asset at an agreed price within a period.

- Swap Contracts

A swap is an agreement between two parties to exchange a series of cash-flows for a set period of time. The series of cashflows can be based on an interest rate, currency rate, equity price or commodity price.

CHAPTER 15

Options

OPTIONS

Options are financial derivatives that give buyers the right, but not the obligation, to buy or sell an underlying asset at an agreed-upon price within a stated period. Call options and put options are the two forms of options. A call option gives the holder the right to buy an asset at an agreed price within a stated period. Put option is the opposite of call option. Put option gives the buyer the right to sell an asset at an agreed price within a period. Options are used to hedge a stock or a portfolio of stocks. There are over the counter (OTC) options and exchange traded options. While the features of OTC options can be negotiated between the parties, exchange traded options have standardized features such as exercise price, expiry dates, volume of an option contract, etc;. Since options have a limited life, they are known as 'wasting assets'. If not used within the stipulated time, they expire unused. Calls are attractive to investors who think a near-term rise in the price, but who prefer not to buy the stock itself. Likewise puts are attractive to investors who anticipate a near-term decline in price, but who prefer not to sell short the stock. The premium is the price of an option. The two factors contributing to the price of an option are the intrinsic value – or the dollar amount by which the stock price exceeds the exercise price of the option and the time value of the option, which is higher the farther away it is from the expiration time. Option premiums are greatly affected by interest rates, tending to be higher when interest rates are high and lower when interest rates are low. Puts are usually cheaper than calls because there is less buyer demand for them. Remember investors are more often bulls than bears. Likewise calls are more expensive in bull markets; and puts are more expensive in bear markets. Black and Scholes formula for option valuation is the widely accepted option valuation method. Options can be used to hedge an asset or a portfolio of assets. Options are available on stocks, currencies, market indexes, bonds, and several other assets. The U.S market is the most advanced for the use of options. In the Indian market, options cannot be sold or purchased on any and every stock. SEBI has permitted options trading on only certain stocks that meet the stringent criteria stipulated by them. The use of options can limit losses through the purchase of puts and increase gains by the sale of puts or the purchase of calls. Sophisticated investors use complex option strategies for return enhancement.

1. All-or-None Order (AON)

A type of option order which requires that the order be executed completely or not at all

2. American-style Option

An option that can be exercised at any time prior to its expiration date

3. Arbitrage

A trading technique that involves the simultaneous purchase and sale of identical assets or equivalent assets in two different markets with the intention to profit from price discrepancy

4. Ask Price

The price at which a seller is offering to sell an option

5. Assigned (Exercised)

Received notification of an assignment (exercise) of an option

6. Assignment

Notification to a clearing member by an exchange/options clearing corporation that an owner of an option has exercised his rights

7. At-the-money option

When the strike price of an option is equal to the market price of the stock, the option is called At-the-money option.

8. Average down

Buying more of a stock or option at a lower price than the original purchase price to reduce the average cost

9. Bearish Spread

An option strategy involving two or more options that can potentially profit from a fall in the price of the underlying stock

10. Bear Put Spread

The simultaneous purchase of one put option with a higher strike price and writing another put option with a lower strike price

11. Bermuda Option

A Bermuda option is a type of exotic options which can be exercised only on specific dates – on a specific day in a month.

12. Bid Price

The price at which a buyer is willing to buy an option

13. Black Monday

Black Monday refers to October 19, 1987 when the Dow Jones Industrial average fell by 22%. This decline marked the beginning of a stock market decline.

14. Black Friday

Black Friday is the day after the US thanksgiving holiday. The day is famous for large discounts in the stores and for the beginning of holiday shopping season.

15. Black-Scholes Formula

The first widely used model for option pricing

16. Break-even Point

The stock price at which an option strategy results in neither a profit nor a loss

17. Bull Call Spread

A bull call spread is an option strategy designed to benefit from a stock's limited increase in price. The strategy uses two call options to create a range consisting of a lower strike price and an upper strike price.

18. Business-to-Business (B2B)

Business-to-Business is a type of transaction between a manufacturer and wholesaler, or wholesaler and retailer.

19. Business-to-Consumer (B2C)

The process of selling goods and services between a business and consumers, who are the end users.

20. Butterfly Spread

An option strategy involving three strike prices with both limited risk and limited profit potential

21. Buy-Write

A covered call position that includes a stock purchase and simultaneous writing of an equivalent number of calls

22. Calendar Spread

An option strategy involving the purchase of a longer-term option (Call or put) and the writing of an equal number of nearer–term option of the same type and strike price

23. Call Option

An option contract that gives the holder the right but not the obligation to buy the underlying stock at a specified price for a fixed period. For the writer of the call option it is an obligation to sell the stock if the option is assigned.

24. Carry

Refers to the interest expense on money borrowed to finance a securities position

25. CBOE

Chicago Board of Options

26. Closing Transaction

The closing of an open option position by an offsetting purchase or sale

27. Collar

A collar is an options strategy that involves buying a downside put and selling an upside call that is implemented to protect against large losses, but that also limits large upside gains.

28. Contract Size

The amount of the underlying asset covered by the option contract

29. Cover

To close out an open position in an option

30. Covered Call Option

An option strategy of writing a call option against the stock that you own. For example, you own 100 shares of ABC and you write 1 ABC December 80 calls.

31. Covered Combination

A strategy in which one call and one put with same expiration month, but different strike prices are written on a stock you hold.

32. Covered straddle

An option strategy in which one call and one put with the same strike price and expiration are written on an underlying stock

33. Cycle

The expiration dates applicable to the different series of options

34. Day Order

An option order good for the day

35. Day Trade

An option position that is opened and closed on the same day

36. Decay

A term used to describe how the theoretical value of an option declines with the passage of time

37. Delivery

The process of meeting the terms of a written option, when the notice of assignment is received. For example, if you receive notice of assignment of a call option that you wrote, you have to deliver the stock on which the call was written and receive cash in settlement thereof.

38. Delta

A measure of the rate of change in an option's theoretical value for one unit change in the price of the underlying stock

39. Derivative

Derivative is a contract that derives its value from the performance of an underlying security.

40. Early Exercise

An American – style option permits the owner to exercise an option at any time prior to the expiration

41. European – style Option

A European – style option is a type of options contract that restricts the exercise prior to expiration date. Because of this restriction, an investor would not be able to take advantage of an appreciation in the underlying stock before the expiry date of the option.

42. Exercise

In a call option, the option owner buys the underlying stock. In the case of a put option, the owner sells the underlying stock.

43. Exercise Price

Exercise price, or strike price, is the price at which the owner of a call option can purchase a stock or the owner of a put option can sell the underlying stock.

44. Expiration Date

The date on which an option expires

45. Expiration Month

The month during which the expiration date falls

46. Fill-or-Kill Order (FOK)

An option order that requires a complete execution. It is similar to an all-or-none (AON) order.

47. Floor Broker

A broker or trader on the floor of an exchange who executes orders for customers

48. Floor Trader

An exchange member on the trading floor who buys and sells for their own account

49. Gamma

The rate of change in an option's Delta for one-unit change in the price of the underlying stock

50. Good-Till-Cancelled (GTC) Order

An order that is valid until execution or cancellation

51. Hedged Position

A position in a stock that is hedged against adverse price move. For example, an owner of XYZ stock may buy a put option to hedge against a possible decline in the price of the stock.

52. Horizontal Spread

An option strategy of purchasing a farther-term call or put option and writing an equal number of nearer-term option of the same type and strike price. For example, buying 1 option of ABC June 100 call and writing 1 ABC March 100 call.

53. Implied Volatility

Implied volatility is the expected volatility of a stock over the life of the option.As expectations change, option premiums react appropriately. Implied volatility is directly influenced by the supply and demand of the underlying options and by the market's expectation of the share price's fluctuation.

54. Index Option

An option on a market index. For example, a call option on S&P 500 index.

55. In-the-money Option (ITM)

When an option has intrinsic value, it is known as in-the-money option. A call option is in-the-money when the stock price is above the strike price. A put option is in-the-money when the stock price is below the strike price.

56. Intrinsic Value

Intrinsic value is the amount by which the strike price of an option is profitable or in-the-money as compared to the market price of the underlying stock. For example, if stock ABC's market price is 100 and the strike price of a call on the stock is 90, the option has an intrinsic value of 10.

57. Limit Order

An order to buy or sell an option at a specific price

58. Listed Option

An option listed/traded on an exchange

59. Long Option Position

The position of an option purchaser which gives the right to buy the stock (in the case of a call) or to sell the stock (in the case of a put) at a specified price (Strike price) at a specified date (expiration date).

60. Long Stock Position

A position when an investor has purchased and owns the stock

61. Margin

Refers to the minimum equity needed to buy a stock. To buy on margin means borrowing part of the purchase price of a security from a brokerage firm.

62. Market Maker

An exchange member on the trading floor who buys and sells options for their own account. A market maker is responsible for maintaining an orderly market.

63. Market Order

An order placed with a broker to immediately buy or sell a stock or option at the best available market price.

64. Market Quote

Market quote refers to the best bid/ask prices for an option or stock on the trading floor of an exchange.

65. Market-not-held Order

A type of market order which gives discretion to the floor broker regarding the price and time of execution.

66. Market-on-close Order

An option order to execute the order at or near the close of trading on the day the order is placed

67. Mark-to-market

The process by which the securities held in an account are valued each day to reflect the closing price

68. Naked Option

Naked option is a short option position that is not fully collateralized if the assignment notice is received. A short call position is naked or uncovered if the writer doesn't own the stock when assignment is received. Naked options run the risk of large loss from sharp price changes before expiration. For example, a trader sells a call option at a strike price of $80 at a premium of $5 but does not own the underlying stock, which makes the option naked. If the stock rises to $100 on expiry date, the trader has to buy it from the market at the current market price of $100. The trader incurs a loss of $20 ($100 - $80), in this case, less the premium received of $5.

69. Neutral Strategy

An option strategy aimed at benefiting from a neutral market outcome

70. Not-Held- Order

A not-held-order gives the broker the time and price discretion to seek the best price available

71. Offer Price

The price at which a seller is offering to sell an option

72. Open Interest

The total number of outstanding option contracts for a given underlying stock

73. Opening Transaction

An opening option transaction creates a trading position.

74. Option

A contract that gives the owner the right, but not the obligation, to buy or sell an underlying stock at a stipulated price for a specified period

75. Option Period

The time period from the creation of an option to its expiration date

76. Option Writer

The option writer is the seller of an option contract who is obligated to meet the delivery terms if the option is assigned on him

77. Optionable Stock

A stock on which listed options are traded

78. Options Clearing Corporation (OCC)

Options Clearing Corporation (OCC) is the world's largest organization for clearing equity derivatives. OCC is based in Chicago. It specializes in equity derivatives clearing, providing central counterparty clearing and settlement services to 16 exchanges.

79. OTC Option

An option traded in the over-the-counter market

80. Out - of - the-money Option (OTM)

An option which has no intrinsic value

81. Parity

When an option contract's premium and its intrinsic value are same, it is in parity.

82. Premium

The premium is the total price of an option, which includes the intrinsic value and time premium.

83. Put Option

An option contract that gives the owner the right to sell the underlying stock at a specified price (strike price) within a period of time (expiry date).

84. Rho

A measure of the expected change in an option's theoretical value for 1% change in interest rates.

85. Secured Put

An option strategy in which a put option is written against the security of sufficient amount of cash to buy the stock if the short option is assigned.

86. Short Option Position

If an investor writes an option, he has an obligation to meet the terms of the option if its owner exercises it. The writer can terminate this obligation by buying back the position through a closing purchase transaction.

87. Specialist

An exchange member whose function is to maintain a fair and orderly market in a given stock or option

88. Straddle

Straddle is an options strategy involving the purchase of both a put and call option for the same expiration date and strike price on the same underlying security. Basically it is a neutral strategy. The strategy is profitable only when the stock either rises or falls from the strike price by more than the total premium paid.

89. Strike price

The strike price is the price at which an Options contract can be exercised. It is the price at which an Option buyer will buy or sell an underlying asset if he wishes to exercise his right.

90. Synthetic Option

A synthetic option is a method of recreating the payoff and risk profile of a particular option position by using combinations of the underlying asset and different options. A synthetic call is created by a long position in the underlying stock combined with a long position in an at-the-money put option. A synthetic put is created by a short position in the underlying stock combined with a long position in an at-the-money call option.

91. Theoretical Option Pricing Model

An option pricing model to calculate the theoretical value of an option using current stock price, expected dividend, the strike price, expected interest rates, time to expiration, and expected stock volatility.

92. Theta

Theta is a measure of the rate at which an option loses its time value as the expiration date draws near. In other words, it is the rate of decline in the option price over time.

93. Time Decay

Denotes how the theoretical value of an option erodes with the passage of time. Time decay is measured by Theta.

94. Time Spread

Time spread refers to an options strategy that involves the purchase of a farther-term option (call or put) and writing of an equal number of nearer-term option of the same type and strike price. For example, buying 1 ABC June 100 call and writing 1 ABC March 100 call. This is also known as calendar spread or horizontal spread.

95. Time Value

An option's total price that exceeds its intrinsic value

96. Trading Pit

A specific location on the trading floor of an exchange where the trading of a specific option takes place

97. Uncovered Call Option Writing

Writing a call option on a stock, in which the writer does not own an equivalent position of the underlying stock

98. Uncovered Put Option Writing

An options strategy in which the investor sells put options without having a short position in the underlying security.

99. Vega

Vega is the measure of an option's sensitivity to implied volatility. It is the change in the option's price for a one-point change in implied volatility.

100. Vertical Spread

Refers to the purchase of one option and writing of another where both are of the same type and same expiration month, but have different strike prices. For example, buying 1 ABC June 90 call and writing 1 ABC June 100 call.

101. Volatility

Volatility is a measure of stock price fluctuations.

102. Write

In option terminology, write means to sell an option through an opening transaction. An investor who so sells an option is called the writer. The writer is under obligation to fulfill the terms of the option, in case the option is assigned.

103. ABC/XYZ Corporation

ABC/XYZ used in the glossary is for a fictitious company used as the underlying stock.

CHAPTER 16

Futures

FUTURES

In Finance, a Futures contract is a standardized legal contract to buy or sell an asset at a predetermined price for delivery at a specified time in the future, between two parties. The asset transacted is usually a commodity or a financial security. The buyer must purchase and the seller must sell the underlying asset at the set price at the predetermined future date. The underlying assets include physical commodities such as oil, agricultural products, metals, livestock, market indices, and financial instruments. Futures contracts are used to hedge against the price movement of an underlying asset or to speculate on the price movement of an asset or commodity. There are several types of futures contracts: Commodity futures (such as crude oil, natural gas, corn, wheat, soybeans, and so on), Stock index futures, Currency futures, Precious metal futures and U.S Treasury futures.

1. Clearing

The procedure through which a clearing house becomes the buyer to each seller of a futures contract and the seller to each buyer.

2. Clearing Firm

A company that works directly through an exchange's clearing house to execute trades on behalf of futures market participants.

3. Clearing House

The division of a futures exchange that settles all trades through an exchange

4. Commodity

A product or physical commodity approved for trading in accordance with the rules of the exchange

5. Commodity Futures Trading Commission (CFTC)

The independent governmental organization that oversees futures and options trading in the United States

6. Contract

A legally binding agreement between two or more parties

7. Contract for Differences (CFD)

A Contract for differences (CFD) is a financial contract to settle the differences between the opening and closing prices of a security trade. CFDs are available for many assets such as commodities, FX contracts, and shares. CFDs are cash settled and hence with a small margin, one can take larger exposure.

8. Counterparty

The party on the opposite side of any trade

9. Delivery

The change of ownership of a commodity on the expiry date of the futures contract

10. Derivative

A futures or options contract, whose value is based on a physical commodity or a financial instrument,

11. Electronic Trading

The carrying out of a trade through computerized processes

12. Exchange

A central market place where buyers and sellers trade futures and options

13. Execution

The completion of an order to buy or sell a futures contract

14. Financial Future

A futures contract on a stock index, interest rates, or foreign exchange rates

15. Limit Order

A purchase order showing the maximum price to pay and a sale order with minimum price to sell

16. Liquidity

The ease of executing an order quickly and efficiently

17. Long

An investor who has bought futures contracts or own a cash commodity

18. Long Hedge

The purchase of a futures contract in anticipation of an actual purchase of the underlying commodity in the cash market

19. Long Option Value

The current market value of all long positions in a trading account

20. Maintenance Margin

Maintenance margin is the minimum amount of equity that an investor has to maintain in the margin account after the purchase is made.

21. Managed Futures

An investment where a portfolio of futures contracts is actively managed by commodity trading advisors

22. Margin

The cash amount a customer has to deposit with the broker for each contract as a sign of his good faith in fulfilling the contract terms

23. Margin Call

A call from a broker to his customer to deposit cash up to the required amount as per exchange rules. Failure to meet margin call may result in the liquidation of the trader's positions without prior notice.

24. Mark to Market (MTM)

In futures trading, futures contract positions in the account are marked to market on a daily basis. Profit and loss are calculated between the long and short positions.

25. Market Maker

A dealer who regularly quotes both bid and ask prices and is ready to make a two way market for any financial instrument.

26. Market Order

An order to buy or sell a specified commodity, at the best possible price when the order is placed

27. Maximum Price Fluctuation

The maximum amount a contract price can change up or down during a trading session, as per exchange rules.

28. Net Asset Value

The value of each unit in a commodity pool, by marking to market all assets and liabilities

29. Net Liquidating Value

Net liquidating value represents how much the contents of a portfolio are worth if all positions are liquidated at current market price.

30. Offer Price

The price at which a futures contract is willing to be sold

31. Open Interest

The outstanding number of futures contracts that are not yet offset

32. Open Order

An order to the broker which is good-till-cancelled

33. Open Outcry

A method of public auction for making bids and offers in the trading pits of futures exchanges

34. Opening Price

The price at which a trade opens at the futures exchange on a trading session

35. Pit

The area on the trading floor of an exchange where futures contracts are bought and sold

36. Position Limit

The maximum number of futures contract one can hold as per exchange regulations

37. Round Turn

Procedure by which a long or short position is offset by an opposite transaction

38. Scalping

Trading a position for a small gain, normally buying and selling a position quickly

39. Segregated Account

A special account used to segregate a customer's assets from those of the broker

40. Single Stock Futures

Futures contracts on individual security

41. Spot Price

Refers to a cash market price for a physical commodity for immediate delivery

42. Switching

Liquidating an existing futures position on a commodity and reinstating that position in another contract month

CHAPTER 17

Convertible Bonds

CONVERTIBLE BONDS

A convertible bond is a type of bond that can be converted into shares of stock of the issuing company. Convertible bonds are typically issued by companies that are looking to raise capital and the interest rates on such bonds are lower than normal bonds, because of the convertible feature. Convertible bonds offer investors the opportunity to receive a higher rate of return than they would receive on a traditional bond. While it would appear that convertibles are an ideal investment medium, providing stable income, capital gains potential, and cushion against stock market declines, the case is not so certain. The analysis of investment merits of convertibles is quite complex. The issuer has to consider a number of factors for issuing convertibles – coupon rate, conversion price and time span for conversion. The investor also has to consider a large number of factors. In analyzing a convertible issue, the investor has to analyse factors such as credit quality of the issuer, interest rate environment, bond value of the issue, conversion features, the time period for conversion, and so on. In short, a convertible is a hybrid security, the price of which is sensitive to interest rate changes, the price of the underlying stock, the issuer's credit rating and the stock market environment.

1. Accrued Interest

Accrued interest is the value of the accrued portion of the coupon on a convertible bond.

2. Anti-dilution provision

The provision for adjustment in the terms of conversion, in the event of special stock dividends, stock splits or other corporate events that can result in the dilution of the underlying share price.

3. At-the-Money (ATM)

A convertible bond is said to be at-the-money when the current share and the conversion price are very close.

4. Bond Floor

The bond floor is the value of the fixed income element of a convertible bond if the conversion rights are excluded.

5. Call Feature

The call feature of a convertible bond gives the issuer a right to redeem the convertible before the maturity at a price set at the time of issue. Holders of the convertible who receive such call notice will have to exercise their right of conversion before repayment takes place.

6. Clean Price

The clean price of a convertible is the price quoted excluding accrued interest.

7. Clean-up Call

If certain percentage of a convertible bond has already been converted into shares, the issuer is entitled to call the remaining bonds, and it is known as a clean-up call.

8. Contingent Conversion

If an investor can convert a convertible contingent upon the share price attaining a specified level, it is called contingent conversion.

9. Conversion Premium

The conversion premium is an amount by which the market price of a convertible bond exceeds the current market value of the common stock into which it may be converted. A conversion premium is an added value that a convertible security possesses due to its conversion option.

10. Conversion Price

Conversion price is the price at which convertible bond can be converted into shares of the issuing company.

Conversion price = Par Value/ Conversion ratio

11. Conversion Ratio

The conversion ratio is the number of shares into which each bond can be converted.

Conversion Ratio = Par Value/Conversion Price

12. Convertible Preferred

Convertible issued in the form of preferred shares. They pay a fixed dividend equivalent to a coupon.

13. Convertible Price

This is the market price of the convertible bond.

14. Coupon

The coupon is the interest payment per bond, which is quoted as a percentage of par.

15. Cross Currency Convertible

A convertible denominated in a different currency to that of the underlying shares

16. Current Yield

It is calculated by dividing the coupon by the convertible price, expressed as a percentage.

17. Delta

Delta is a measure of the sensitivity of the convertible bond price to the share price.

18. Dirty Price

The dirty price of a convertible bond is the clean price plus its accrued interest.

19. Exchangeable Bond

A convertible bond issued by one company which can be converted into the shares of a different company

20. Gamma

Gamma is a measure of the sensitivity of a convertible bond's delta to share price movements.

21. Hedge Ratio

The hedge ratio of a convertible bond shows its equity sensitivity. It helps the investor to find how many shares he would need to sell to hedge the equity exposure.

22. In-the –money

A convertible bond is said to be in–the-money if the current share price is greater than the conversion price

23. Issue Price

The issue price is the price at which a convertible bond is sold to investors at issue.

24. Mandatory Convertible

A convertible bond in which the bondholder is obliged to convert into the underlying equity

25. Maturity

The final redemption date of the bond

26. Original Issue Bond (OID)

A convertible bond issued at a discount to the par

27. Out- of-the-money

A convertible is out-of-the-money if the current share price is below the conversion price.

28. Par

Par refers to the face value a bond

29. Parity

Parity is the market value of the shares into which the bond may be converted. It is calculated by multiplying the conversion ratio by the current share price, expressed as a percentage of a bond's nominal value.

30. Premium

A convertible's premium is the percentage by which the market price of the convertible bond exceeds parity.

31. Put option feature

The Option to the investor to sell back the convertible bond to the issuer at a fixed price on a given date

32. Rho

Rho is a measure of the sensitivity of the convertible price to movements in interest rates.

33. Step-up Coupon

This is, where the coupon on a convertible bond increases in future due to an event such as a bond downgrade

34. Theta

Theta is a measure of the change in the convertible value with the passage of time.

35. Vega

Vega is a measure of the change in the convertible price due to changes in the volatility of the underlying stock.

36. Yield Advantage

The yield advantage is the difference between the current yield of the convertible bond and the dividend yield of the stock.

CHAPTER 18

Preference Shares

PREFERENCE SHARES

Preference Shares are shares of a company's stock with dividends that are paid out to shareholders before common stock dividends are issued. As the name indicates preference shareholders have a preference over holders of common stock. Preferred shares are more commonly referred to as preferred stock. Most preference shares have affixed dividend, while common stocks generally do not. Preferred stock shareholders do not enjoy voting rights, while common shareholders do. Preference shares are ideal for risk-averse investors. Preference shares show characteristics similar to both common shares and a fixed-income security. If the company enters bankruptcy, preferred stockholders are entitled to be paid from company assets before common stockholders. There are several types of preference shares.

1. Adjustable Preference Shares

Adjustable preference shares are those shares for which the dividend rate is not fixed and is adjustable by current market rates.

2. Convertible Preference Shares

Convertible Preference shares are those shares that can be easily converted into equity shares.

3. Cumulative Preference Shares

Cumulative preference shares are those type of shares that give the shareholders the right to receive cumulative dividend payout from the company even if they do not make profit. The unpaid dividends will be counted as arrears during the years when the company is not making profit and will be paid on a cumulative basis when the company generates profits.

4. Dividend Preference

When it comes to dividends, preference shareholders are entitled to dividends before common shareholders are paid.

5. Non-Convertible Preference Shares

Non-convertible preference shares are those shares which cannot be converted into equity shares.

6. Non-Cumulative Preference Shares

Non-cumulative preference shareholders are not entitled for dividends when the company doesn't make profits. In other words they are not entitled to cumulative dividends.

7. Non-Participating Preference Shares

Non-participating preference shares are entitled only for fixed dividends and do not enjoy any additional dividends from the surplus profits earned by the company.

8. Non-Redeemable Preference Shares

Non-redeemable preference shares are those shares that cannot be redeemed by the issuing company.

9. Participating Preference Shares

Participating preference shares are those shares entitled to surplus profits of the company at the time of company's liquidation, in addition to the fixed dividends.

10. Redeemable Preference Shares

Redeemable preference shares are those shares that can be redeemed by the issuing company at a fixed rate on a fixed date.

11. Voting Rights

Preference shareholders do not enjoy voting rights normally, but they are entitled to the right to vote in case of extraordinary events.

12. Preference in Assets

In the case of liquidation, preference shareholders have priority over non-preferential shareholders in the assets of the company.

CHAPTER 19

Currencies

CURRENCIES

A currency is defined as a system of money in general use in a particular country. Currency is used as a medium of exchange for goods and services. In short, it's money, in the form of paper and coins, usually issued by a government, circulated within its jurisdiction and generally accepted at its face value as a method of payment. As we know, currency has replaced the system of bartering long ago. Currency is a tangible form of money, which is an intangible system of value. The value of a country's currency fluctuates in relation to the currency of another country. When we talk of currency, it is U.S.Dollar, that comes to our minds first. Many countries accept the U.S. Dollar for payment, while others peg their currency value directly to the U.S.Dollar. Modern currencies are issued on paper in various denominations, with fractional issues in the form of coins. Coins are made of gold, silver, bronze or an alloy. Money and currency are often thought to mean the same thing. There are over 200 national currencies in circulation currently. Including the United States, 42 countries either use the U.S.Dollar or peg their currencies directly to the dollar. Most countries issue their own currencies. An exception is the "euro", which is issued by the European Central Bank (the national central banks of the Euro-system) and adopted by most countries that are members of the European Union. There are also branded currencies, like airline and credit card points and former Disney Dollars. These are issued by companies and are used only to pay for the products and services to which they are tied. The 21st century witnessed a new form of currency – Cryptocurrency, a digital currency designed to work as a medium of exchange through computer network that is not reliant on any central bank or government authority. The growth of cryptocurrencies and the threat posed by them are forcing central banks to issue their own digital currencies. A central bank digital currency (CBDC) is the digital form of a country's fiat currency. A CBDC is issued and regulated by a nation's monetary authority or central bank.

Foreign exchange is defined as the conversion of one currency into another currency. In other words, it is the exchange of one currency for another. The term Foreign exchange is also known as Forex, FX, or currency. The foreign exchange market refers to the market in which various participants buy and sell currencies. The forex market is very decentralized. The various market participants in the forex market include central banks, banks, financial institutions, sovereign wealth funds, commercial companies, investment firms, forex brokers, hedge funds, and individual investors. The forex market operates around the clock, with the exception of weekends. The global forex market is, by far, the largest financial market – with the average daily volume of trillions of dollars.

1. Adjustable Peg

Some countries have pegged or fixed their currencies to a leading currency, such as the US dollar. However, they readjust the peg from time to time to make the currency more competitive. This arrangement is known as an adjustable peg.

2. Appreciation

A currency is said to appreciate when it strengthens in price against another currency.

3. Arbitrage

Arbitrage is the process of taking advantage of price differentials within different markets by selling or purchasing a currency.

4. Ask Price

Ask price is the price at which a forex trader accepts to buy a particular currency.

5. Authorized Forex Dealer

A dealer is a financial institution that has been authorized by a country's regulatory body to act as such for trading in currencies.

6. Aussie

Refers to AUD/USD pair. This is also called oz or ozzie.

7. Base Currency

The first currency listed in a currency pair is called the "base currency." For example, in a GBP/USD currency pairing, the GBP is the base currency.

8. Bear Market

The term "bear market" is used to describe the price of a currency that is in decline.

9. Bid Price

Bid price is a term used to describe the price at which a forex trader is willing to sell a particular currency.

10. Bitcoin

A digital currency introduced in 2009. It is not regulated by any central bank. Bitcoin is traded on the internet and is based on a peer-to peer network.

11. Bretton Woods Agreement

An agreement established in 1944 at the United Nations Monetary and Financial conference held in Bretton Woods, New Hampshire, United States. The agreement established the adjustable, pegged foreign exchange rate system. Under the Bretton Woods system, gold was the basis for US dollar and other currencies were pegged to the US dollar's value. However, this system came to an end in the 1970s.

12. Bull Market

The term "bull market" is used to describe the price of a currency that is rising.

13. Bureau de Change

An establishment at which customers can exchange foreign currency

14. Cable

Cable is a slang term to denote the GBP/USD currency pair. It is mainly used by forex traders.

15. Closing Market Rate

Closing market rate or closing price is the final price at which a currency is traded during a day.

16. Commodity Currencies

Currencies of countries that are based on natural resources. Examples are Canadian dollar, Australian dollar, and the New Zealand dollar.

17. Contract for Differences (CFD)

A contract for differences is a financial contract that pays the differences in the settlement price between the open and closing trades. CFDs allow investors to trade the direction of securities in the short-term. Mainly CFDs are used for trading FX and commodity products. The CFDs are cash settled.

18. Currency Appreciation

Currency appreciation is the rise in the value of one currency against another.

19. Currency Code

The three - letter code representing a currency. The codes are those issued by the International Standards Organization. Examples are: US dollar - USD, Japanese Yen - JPY, Indian Rupee – INR, etc

20. Currency Futures

Currency futures are contracts that state the price at which a currency can be sold or bought at a future date.

21. Currency Pair

Currency pairs are the national currencies from two countries coupled for trading. All trading within the forex market, whether selling or buying, will take place through currency pairs.

22. Day Trade

A forex trade that is opened and closed on the same day

23. Dealing Spread

The difference between the buying and selling price of a currency pair. It is also called the bid-offer spread.

24. Delivery Date (Settlement Date)

The date on which both buyer and seller of a currency trade make physical delivery of the currencies. It is also known as the settlement date.

25. Devaluation

When a pegged currency is allowed to weaken by an official action

26. Dovish

A country's monetary policymakers are dovish, when they believe that easier monetary policy or lower interest rates are needed to boost economic growth.

27. Drawdown

If a currency dips, the difference between the peak and the new low is known as the "drawdown".

28. DXY Index (US dollar Index)

DXY is an index to measure the value of US dollar against the value of six foreign currencies (Euro, Japanese Yen, Pound Sterling, Canadian dollar, Swedish Krona, and Swiss franc). The index was introduced in 1973.

29. Exchange Rate

The exchange rate is the price at which one currency is traded against another.

30. Exposure

Exposure is a term to describe the amount invested in a currency and the market risk arising as a result.

31. Fill or Kill

A forex order, if not executed at the set price, will get terminated

32. Floating Exchange Rate

An exchange rate which fluctuates based on the supply and demand of a particular currency relative to other currencies

33. FOMC

Federal Open Market committee, the policy-setting committee of the US Federal Reserve

34. Foreign Exchange Fixing

The daily monetary exchange rate fixed by the central bank of a country

35. Forex Chart

Forex chart is a digital chart showing the price movements related to a currency pair

36. Forex Scalping

A forex trading strategy involving the buying and selling of a currency within a short space of time to earn a higher profit

37. Forex Spot Rate

The current exchange rate at which a currency pair can be bought or sold, for settlement two business days after the transaction date. It is called **T+2** settlement.

38. Forward Exchange Rate

The forward exchange rate is the exchange rate at which a bank agrees to exchange one currency for another at a future date.

39. Forward Points

The pips added to or subtracted from the current exchange rate in order to calculate a forward rate.

40. Greenback

A nickname for the US dollar

41. Hard Currency

A hard currency is the one that is often most resilient in times of political or economic instability. USD, GBP and EUR are well known hard currencies.

42. Hawkish

A country's monetary policymakers are referred to as hawkish when they believe that higher interest rates are needed to fight inflation.

43. Interbank Rates

The foreign exchange rates quoted between banks

44. Intervention

The intervention of a central bank in the currency market to stabilize a currency's movements or to support the currency from wild swings

45. Intra-day Trade

A forex trade that is opened and closed during the same business day

46. Kiwi

A nickname for the New Zealand dollar

47. Leverage

The facility offered by the forex broker to the trader to trade a high volume of currency against the deposit of a small amount of capital

48. Long Position

Buying a base currency with a view to profiting from a price increase

49. Loonie

A nickname for the Canadian dollar

50. Lot

The standardized quantity of a currency that is tradable

51. Margin

Margin is the minimum account balance required to maintain an open position in a currency

52. Margin Call

A notification to make additional deposit to increase the margin in order to keep trading positions active

53. Market Order

An order to execute a currency trade immediately at the best possible rate

54. Open Position

A position that a trader takes on a currency pair

55. Overnight Position

A position in a currency kept open overnight and carried over to the next trading day

56. Pip

Pip stands "percentage in point", which is the smallest price change possible within an exchange rate. Currency rates are quoted normally with four decimals and pip represents the very last digit. Hence pip is equivalent to 0.0001. For example, if USD/CAD exchange rate were to move from 1.3210 to 1.3211, the change in value can be said as one pip.

57. Profit-Taking

Refers to closing a forex position as a means to book profit in the position

58. Quote Currency

The second currency listed in a currency pair is known as the "quote currency". For example, in the USD/CAD pairing, the CAD is the quote currency.

59. Rally

Rally refers to a currency's recovery after a short decline.

60. Registrar and Transfer Agent (RTA)

Registrar or transfer agents are the trusts or institutions that register and maintain detailed records of the transactions of investors for the convenience of mutual fund houses. Some of the RTAs operating in India are CAMS, Karvy, and Deutsche Investor services.

61. Resistance

Resistance is the price level a currency finds difficult to break and move forward.

62. Revaluation

When a pegged currency is allowed to appreciate by an official action

63. Round Trip

A trade that has been opened and subsequently closed by an equal and opposite deal.

64. Short Position

Short position is a position taken to benefit from a currency's decline.

65. Soft Currency

A soft currency is a currency which is vulnerable to economic and political events. Examples are North Korean Won (KPW) and Venezuelan bolivar (VEF).

66. Spread

In a currency quote, the difference between the bid and ask price is called the spread. In volatile market situations the spread can be wider.

67. Sterling

A nickname for the British pound

68. Stop-Loss Order

Stop loss order is an order to control losses, by buying or selling a currency at a certain price.

69. Street Rate

Black market exchange rate

70. Swap

A currency swap is a transaction in which two parties exchange an equivalent amount of money with each other, but in different currencies. The swap takes place at a specified date at the agreed exchange rate.

71. Swissy

A nickname for the Swiss franc

72. Technical Analysis

Technical analysis is frequently used by investors to forecast exchange rate movements by analyzing historical price charts and other tools.

73. Tick

The minimum change, either up or down, in a currency's exchange rate

74. Tomorrow Next (tom next)

Tomorrow next is a short-term foreign exchange transaction where a currency is simultaneously bought and sold over two separate business days: those being tomorrow and the following day. The purpose is to allow traders and investors to maintain their position without taking physical delivery.

CHAPTER 20

Mutual Funds

MUTUAL FUNDS

A mutual fund is a pool of money managed by a professional fund manager. It is a trust that collects money from a number of investors who share a common investment objective and invests that money in equities, bonds, money market instruments and other financial securities. Mutual funds offer diversification and thus lower the risk in the investments. There are several types of mutual funds depending on their investments, styles and other features. Mutual funds are subject to annual management fees, expenses, or commissions. Investing in a share/unit of mutual fund is different from investing in a share of stock. Unlike stock, mutual fund investors do not enjoy any voting rights. The price of a mutual fund is referred to as net asset value (NAV) per share/unit. NAVs are updated daily and investors can purchase shares at the NAVs. Investors earn income from mutual fund investments through dividends, capital gain from underlying investments and sale of units when they increase in price. The global mutual fund industry was valued at $66 trillion in 2022. Unit Trust of India (UTI) pioneered the mutual fund industry in India in 1963 by launching the first mutual fund " Unit Scheme 1964". Since then the industry witnessed an exponential growth in India with several banks and asset managers entering the industry. Then foreign asset managers entered the scene. Looking back, the Indian mutual fund industry, despite witnessing substantial growth, had its setbacks also.

1. Account Fee

Some mutual funds separately charge investors for the maintenance of their accounts. This fee is called account fee.

2. Asset Management Company (AMC)

Asset management company is the company that manages funds.

3. Assets Under Management (AUM)

It is the total size of assets under the management of a fund manager. AUM fluctuates as new investments are received and redemptions of units are made. The size of AUM is an indication of the manager's capability and the trust of investors in the manager.

4. Balanced Funds

Balanced funds invest across various asset classes, such as stocks, bonds, money market securities, or alternative investments.

5. Benchmark Index

Benchmark index is the index based on which the performance of a fund is measured. All funds have a benchmark to compare the performance.

6. Bond Funds

A mutual fund that generates bulk of its return from fixed income securities. The investments of such funds include government bonds, corporate bonds, and other debt instruments.

7. Custodian

A bank that holds a mutual fund's assets, settles all portfolio trades, and collects all valuation data for the calculation of NAV

8. Cut-Off-Time

The time of a day when transaction (purchase or redemption) can no longer be accepted

9. Dividend

A dividend is a portion of a mutual fund's profit paid to unit holders.

10. Dividend Reinvest

Dividends paid to investors are automatically invested back into the units of a mutual fund. Units are purchased at the fund's net asset value as of the dividend date.

11. Dollar Cost Averaging

Investing the same amount of money at regular intervals in a mutual fund over an extended period of time. This may reduce the average cost of holding if units are purchased at lower prices.

12. Exchange Fee

A fee that some mutual funds charge shareholders if they exchange (transfer) to another mutual fund within the same fund group

13. Expense Ratio

A fund's expense ratio is the summation of the advisory or management fee and its administrative costs, expressed as a percentage of the total fund size, usually ranging between 1-3%.

14. Fixed Maturity Plans (FMP)

Fixed maturity plans are closed ended funds, meaning that the fund remains open for a specific period at issue and after the close no further investments are permitted in the fund

15. Fund Manager

A fund manager, otherwise called as investment advisor, is the investment manager, who is legally obligated to work in the best interest of mutual fund shareholders.

16. Global Funds

Global funds or International funds invest only in assets located outside the home country

17. Income Funds

These funds invest primarily in government and high quality debt securities to get a steady income.

18. Index Funds

Index funds invests in market indexes such as Dow Jones Industrial Average (DJIA) or S&P 500 or stocks that correspond with major market index.

19. Investment Objective

The goal of a mutual fund includes capital growth, income, tax-free income and so on.

20. Lipper Ratings

Lipper Analytical Services of New York rank the performances of mutual funds on a quarterly and annual basis.

21. Load

Any charge collected by a fund on entry and exit. The charge collected at the time of investment is called **Entry load**. The charge collected at the time of redemption is called **Exit load.** The charge represents the administrative and operating expenses of the fund.

22. Money Market Funds

The money market fund is relatively safe and risk free as it invests in Treasury bills, and short-term debt instruments.

23. Net Asset Value (NAV)

In simple terms Net asset value is the price per share or unit of a mutual fund. Net asset value of a fund is calculated at the end of the trading day. It is at the NAV that new issue of units or redemption of units take place.

24. New Fund Offer (NFO)

NFO is an initial offer of a fund, similar to an IPO. The offer is open for a stipulated period at a set unit price (Say, usually Rs.10 in India). After the close of the NFO, an investor can purchase units at the prevailing NAV only.

25. No-Load Fund

A no-load fund is a mutual fund in which shares are sold without commission or sales charge. The reason for this is that the shares are distributed directly by the investment company without the involvement of a secondary party.

26. Open Ended Funds

Open ended mutual funds are always open to investment and redemptions. These funds do not have any lock-in period or maturities. Open ended funds are the most common form of mutual funds in India.

27. Prospectus

A document that describes a mutual fund. The prospectus contains information about a fund's objectives, risks, fund's costs and performance. Each mutual fund has a prospectus. An investor needs to read and understand the prospectus before taking an investment decision.

28. Quant Funds

A Quantitative fund, otherwise called Quant fund, is a fund using mathematical and statistical techniques, as well as automated algorithms and advanced quantitative models, to invest and execute trades.

29. Regional Funds

These funds focus on specific geographic areas

30. Socially Responsible Funds (SRF)

Socially responsible funds invest only in companies that meet certain guidelines, such as green technology, solar or wind energy.

31. Specialty Funds

Specialty funds invest in specific sectors of the economy, such as financial, technology, or healthcare.

32. Stock Funds

Stock fund invests principally in equity or stocks. There are several sub-categories within this group: small cap, mid cap, and large cap. Some funds are named after their investment strategy: aggressive growth, income-oriented, value fund, and others. Then there are domestic funds or universal funds.

33. Systematic Investment Plan (SIP)

SIP gives investors the facility to invest in a mutual fund on a monthly basis in small amounts. Every month new units are purchased by the investor at the prevailing NAV on the day of purchase that is a set date every month (for example, the first day of every month). The investor has to maintain an account with the bank and the amounts gets debited automatically every month. As SIP is made at various NAVs, the investor gets an average cost for his holdings. In case the market falls he gets higher number of units and if market rises, he makes money on previously purchased units.

34. Systematic Transfer Plan (STP)

Systematic Transfer Plan is a mutual fund investment strategy whereby an investor invests the target funds in a fixed income fund of the fund house and transfers periodically the amount, he decides, to the equity fund from the fixed income fund. Thus investment into equity fund is made on a staggered basis.

35. Systematic Withdrawal Plan (SWP)

Systematic withdrawal plan gives investor an option to withdraw his accumulated fund units over a span of time.

CHAPTER 21

Metals

METALS

A metal is a material that, when freshly prepared, polished, or fractured, shows a lustrous appearance. It conducts electricity and heat relatively well. Metals are typically ductile and malleable. Iron, gold, silver, aluminium, copper, and alloys such as steel are examples of familiar types of metals. Most metals are present in the earth as compounds of some sort, such as oxides or sulphides. Most metals are used, one way or another, in all walks of life. Investing in metals in general and base metals in particular is not very difficult. Metal is an interesting raw material as it is possible to invest in it both in the form of securities and in physical form. It can be difficult for the private investor to store a large quantity of metal in the backyard. But it is excellent to have precious metal, such as gold or silver, in your own custody. Many people mistakenly believe that it is only possible to invest in precious metals, such as gold or silver. It is possible to invest in many different metals. Some of them are good hedges against inflation. In addition to precious metals used as a hedge in a portfolio, an investor can also invest in base metal, or industrial metal, for portfolio diversification. There are many different ways to invest in metal. The most common are investments in securities linked to the underlying metal. They include the shares of companies like

US Steel, futures, options, and ETFs. Precious metals also offer investment opportunities through shares of mining companies, ETFs, options and futures. Investors are also getting interested in the shares of rare earth producing companies and related ETFs. However, trading in securities is still the most common and easiest way to invest in metals. In this chapter the jargons associated with select precious metals are discussed. Precious metals are rare metals that have high economic value. They are valuable because they are scarce, useful in industrial processes, or a good store of value. Notable precious metals include gold, silver, platinum, and palladium.

A. Gold is the most popular and investable precious metal. It's unique for its durability, ability to conduct heat and electricity and shaping capability. It has industrial uses in dentistry and electronics. Gold is primarily used to make jewellery or as a form of currency. Gold is seen as a safe haven in times of economic or political uncertainty. More over, gold is a hedge against rising inflation. There are several ways to invest in gold – gold coins, bars, jewellery, gold stocks, gold focused ETFs, and gold focused mutual funds. Each investment option has its pros and cons. Advantages include the ability of holding physical gold to track the precious metal's price. Drawbacks include the expense of storing and insurance. The chemical symbol of Gold is **Au**. The commodity symbol for Gold is **XAU,** which shows the spot price of one ounce of gold in dollar terms. One ounce is 28.3495 grams. There are different channels to invest in gold: physical gold, gold ETFs, gold mutual funds, gold bonds and digital gold. Each channel has its pros and cons.

1. Alloy

A mixture of two elements, at least one of which is a metal, which form a new metal with desired properties

2. Assay

Assay is a biochemical test done on precious metals to determine the content and purity of the object. A buyer of gold has to know the purity of the gold he is buying, and hence the assay.

3. Bar Bullion

A precious metal that is minted and formed into a bar shape

4. Bullion

Physical metal that is minted and shaped for easy storage and transport

5. Coin Bullion

A precious metal that is minted and in the round shape of a coin with a legal trade value.

6. Conductivity

The ability of a mineral to transmit heat, electricity or sound

7. Corrosion

Gradual chemical destruction of a mineral

8. Density

The average mass per unit of volume of a substance

9. Digital Gold

Digital gold is an alternative to buying physical gold. The concept of digital gold is a recent development. Digital gold allows one to invest in 24 Ct., 999.9 purest gold,which is then stored in secure vaults of select digital gold platforms / dealers. MMTC-PAMP, Augmont Goldtech Pvt.Ltd., and Digital Gold India Pvt. Ltd., are the main platforms for digital gold. These companies purchase gold and store them safely in their vaults. You can redeem digital gold for physical gold: coins, bars and bullions. The minimum amount of investment is 1 gram or in some cases Re.1.

10. Ductility

The ability of a mineral to be pulled into wire

11. Electronic Gold Receipt (EGR)

Electronic Gold Receipt (EGR) means depository gold receipts that can be traded on exchanges. They are similar to stocks and can be traded and held in Demat accounts like stocks. Under this form of gold, the trading exchange holds the underlying value of the gold in physical gold in vaults. The Bombay Stock Exchange launched EGRs in October 2022, by issuing two new products of 995 and 999 purity.

12. Fineness

A measure of the amount of pure gold in a metal. The maximum fineness is 0.999 even if the gold is absolutely pure.

13. Gold Eagles

Gold eagles, also called American gold eagles, are 22 karat gold bullion. Eagles are backed by the US government in purity and content. They come in the following weights: tenth of an ounce, quarter ounce, half ounce, and whole ounce.

14. Gold Maple Leaf

Gold maple leaf, also called Canadian gold maple leaves, are 24 karat gold bullions made by 12 the royal Canadian mint. They come in the following weights: twentieth of an ounce (1/20 oz), tenth of an ounce (1/10 oz), quarter ounce (1/4 oz), half ounce(1/2 oz), and whole ounce.

15. Gold Standard

A system in which currency can be redeemed for a fixed amount of gold

16. Hallmarking

Hallmarking is a purity certification of gold jewellery. Hallmarking of jewellery is mandatory in India since January 15, 2021.

17. Ingot

Large gold bars that are produced by pouring the liquid hot metal into molds

18. Karat

Karat, also spelled Carat, is a measure of the amount of pure gold in a metal. One Karat is 1/24th of the total weight of the object. Karat is measured on a scale from 0 to 24, with 24 Karat being the purest gold. Hundred percent pure gold (99.99%) is 24 Karat, but it is brittle and hence 24Ct ornaments are not popular. Ornaments are mainly 22Ct (22/24= 0.916) and 21Ct (21/24=0.875). 22Ct and 21Ct gold are identified by the hallmarking of 916 and 875 on such ornaments. The amount of copper added to 24Ct gold determines 22Ct and 21 Ct. Copper is added to gold to make it more strong and durable. In U.S. English Karat is used for purity of gold, while in other countries Carat is used. In the U.S. Carat represents a measure of diamond, taking its weight into consideration.

19. Kruggerand

A gold bullion coin first minted by the government of South Africa in 1967 and are 22 karat gold.

20. Malleability

A mineral's ability to be hammered into thin sheets

21. Mining Stock

Stock of a mining company that is publicly traded.

22. Nugget

A lump of gold found in nature

23. Ore

Rock from which valuable minerals can be extracted

24. Rose Gold

Rose gold is an alloy made from a combination of pure gold and copper in the proportion of 75% pure gold and 25% copper. The blend of the two metals change the colour of the final product and its karat to 18Ct. The final product has a pinkish colour and hence the name 'rose gold'.

25. Sovereign Gold Bond Scheme (SGB)

Sovereign Gold Bond scheme (SGB) is a scheme introduced by the Government of India to facilitate investment in gold. SGBs are **government securities denominated in grams of gold**. They are substitutes for holding physical gold. Investors have to pay the issue price in cash and the bonds will be redeemed in cash on maturity. There will be interest receivable on the bond. SGB is issued by RBI on behalf of the government. The issue price and redemption price depend on the price of gold as per the IBJA Rate. IBJA stands for India Bullion and Jewellers Association. This is an alternative investment method to benefit from gold price changes, without physically holding gold.

26. Troy Ounce (ozt)

One Troy ounce is equivalent to 31.1034768 grams. A standard ounce is equivalent to 28.349 grams. The Troy ounce is the last remaining metric still used in the troy weighting system.

27. White Gold

White gold is an alloy mixed with palladium or nickel.

28. Yellow Gold

Yellow gold is the purest form in gold, and for jewellery, it is made into alloy which contains pure gold, zinc, and copper.

B. Silver

Silver is a precious shiny grayish-white metal. It is very ductile, malleable and brilliant. Silver has the highest electrical and thermal conductivity of any metal. It is used in jewellery, tableware, cutlery, coinage, electroplating and in electrical contacts. Precious metals such as silver have long been an alternative to traditional investments. Silver is used by investors as an inflation hedge. In addition, many see it as a store of value. There are a number of ways to invest in silver: own it outright or own shares in companies who produce it. The chemical symbol of Silver is Ag and the ticker symbol for spot Silver (one oz) vs. dollar is XAG.

C. Copper

Copper is a soft, malleable, and ductile metal with very high thermal and electrical conductivity. Copper is used as a conductor of heat and electricity, as a building material, and as a constituent of various metal alloys. The chemical symbol is **Cu.** The commodity ticker is **HG** and the price quoted on **NASDAQ** is per lb in dollar terms.

D. Palladium

Palladium is a rare and lustrous silvery-white metal, with many uses in electrical contacts, dental alloys, jewellery, and other uses. Small amount of palladium alloyed with gold produce the best white gold. The chemical symbol is **Pd.** The easiest way to invest in Palladium is through palladium –focused exchange- traded- funds (SPPP or PALL).

CHAPTER 22

Oil

OIL

Oil is an economically crucial resource, providing the bulk of energy for transportation as well as raw materials for manufacturing. It is the world's most heavily traded commodity. An Oil is a chemical substance that is composed of hydrocarbons. Oil is both hydrophobic (does not mix with water) and lipophilic (mixes with other oils). Oils are inflammable. Oils may be petrochemical, animal, or vegetable in origin. They are used for fuel, lubrication, food, medical use, and for manufacture of paints, plastics, and other materials. Of all the types of oil, crude oil comes to our minds first, as it is an important resource for the world economy. The word oil comes from old French oile, from Latin oleum.

How to Invest in Oil

Investors have several ways to invest in crude oil. The investment venues range from crude oil futures and options to exchange traded derivatives, energy equities, and sector mutual funds. Each of the aboveth, while giving exposure to one of world's most volatile commodities, has its own risks too. Oil prices are set principally by its supply-demand factors. In addition, political factors also influence oil price. Crude oil price is generally very volatile. Hence a great amount of caution and discipline is warranted while deciding to invest in crude oil.

1. Crude

Brent is the name given to a relatively light crude oil made from a blend of crudes from 19 oil fields in the North Sea. Brent Crude is one of the three main benchmarks for crude oil prices per barrel, along with WTI and Dubai Crude from the Persian Gulf.

2. Cooking Oil

Edible vegetable oils are used for various purposes in cooking and food preparation.

3. Cosmetics Oil

Oils are used in various cosmetic applications including as a hair conditioner.

4. Diesel

Diesel fuel is the common term for the distillate fuel used in motor vehicles.

5. Dubai Crude

Dubai Crude is a medium sour crude oil extracted from Dubai. Dubai Crude is used as a benchmark for oil price, in addition to WTI and Brent Crude.

6. Fuel

Fuel oil is any of the various fractions obtained from the distillation of petroleum (crude oil). Fuel oil is used for different things and is known by different names such as Diesel fuel, Kerosene oil, or Furnace oil

7. Heat Transfer

Oils are used as coolants in oil cooling.

8. Lubrication

Oils are used as lubricants for various engineering purposes.

9. Mineral Oil

Mineral oil is particularly a distillate of petroleum. Crude oil or petroleum originates from ancient fossilized organic materials.

10. OPEC

The Organization of the Petroleum Exporting Countries is an inter-governmental organization of 13 petroleum producing countries. OPEC plays a crucial role in the control of oil production and its supply in order to ensure a fair price for producers and a regular supply of petroleum to consumers. OPEC is also called an Oil Cartel.

11. Organic Oil

Organic oils are produced by plants, animals, and other organisms through natural metabolic processes.

12. Painting

Oil is a supporting medium for paints as colour pigments are easily soluble in oil.

13. Petrodollar

Petrodollar refers to U.S. dollars earned by oil-exporting countries in settlement of oil exported by them. As dollar is the most widely used currency, OPEC and other oil exporters have used U.S.dollar as the settlement currency for their oil exports, making it easier for them to invest the export proceeds.

14. Petrol

Petrol is a light fuel oil that is obtained by distilling petroleum and used in internal combustion engines. It is mainly used as a fuel for cars and other motor vehicles.

15. Petroyuan

Petroyuan refers to money earned in Chinese Yuan from the sale of oil. As an alternative to the U.S.dollar as the settlement currency for the import of oil, China have agreed with some oil exporting countries such as Saudi Arabia and Russia to settle oil purchases in Chinese yuan instead of the US dollar.

16. Religion

Oil has been used in various religions as a purifying agent and for anointing purposes for many years. For example, anointing oil and olive oil have been important ritual liquids for Judaism and Christianity. Similarly ghee or castor oil is an essential part of pooja oil in Hinduism.

17. West Texas Intermediate (WTI)

WTI is a blend of US crude oils, drilled and processed in the United States. WTI is primarily a benchmark for the US oil market.

CHAPTER 23

Islamic Investments

ISLAMIC INVESTMENTS

Islamic investments are a unique form of investments. Islamic investing is different from traditional investing, because in order to be compliant, managers and investors need to adhere to Shari'ah law. Shari'ah refers to the divine counsel that Muslims follow to live moral lives and grow close to God, and hadith – thousands of sayings and practices attributed to Prophet Mohammed. The giving and receiving of interest (riba), extremely risky investments, gambling, prostitution, and alcohol consumption are prohibited in Islam. The belief that trade is to be conducted in a faithful and beneficial manner and the principle of risk-sharing form the basis of Islamic business.

AAOIFI

Accounting and Auditing Organization for Islamic Financial Institutions (AAOIFI) is an organization established to maintain and promote Shari'ah standards for Islamic financial institutions, participants, and the overall industry. AAOIFI defines the acceptable standards for various functions, including accounting, governance, ethics, transactions, and investment. In Islamic banking, collection of interest (riba) is forbidden, and sharing of profits and losses amongst the community is mandated.

Islamic Finance Basics

There are two fundamental principles of Islamic (shari'ah) banking. They are (1) the sharing of profit and loss, and (2) the prohibition of the collection and payment of interest by lenders and investors. To earn money without the use of charging interest, Islamic banks use the system of equity participation. Equity participation means if a bank loans money to a business, the business will pay back the loan without interest, but instead gives the bank a share in its profits. If the business doesn't earn a profit, then the bank also does not benefit from the loan.

Shari'ah

Sharia, spelled in Arabic as shari'ah, refers to a set of Islamic religious law that governs aspects of day-to-day life for Muslims in addition to religious rituals. Shari'ah law provides the guidelines for Muslims to take decisions in their lives, such as finances, banking and investments. Interest is haram under shari'ah law, which means it is prohibited for interest to be paid between borrowers and lenders. Investing in conventional banking and conventional insurance is forbidden under shari'ah. Business activities such as brewing alcohol, pornography, pork products, tobacco related activities, gambling, and production of weapons, are prohibited in shari'ah law.

The important jargons used in Islamic investments are introduced below:

1. Al Ajr

This refers to commission, reward, remuneration, fees or wages charged for services

2. Amana / Amanah

This means deposits held in trust. A person may hold property in trust for another.

3. Al Rahn

This refers to an arrangement of placing a valuable asset as collateral for a debt. In case of a default, the collateral may be disposed off to satisfy the debt.

4. Al Wadiah

Al Wadiah means amanat (Bailment) or safe keeping.

5. Bai Muajjal

Bai Muajjal means a Deferred Payment Contract, which involves the sale of goods on a deferred payment basis. The bank or the provider of capital buys the goods on behalf of a business owner and then sells the goods to the client at an agreed price. The agreed price will include a mark-up which is the bank's profit. The business owner can make payment to the bank as per an agreed schedule.

6. Bai Al-Arboon

This is a sale agreement involving payment of an advance deposit as a partial payment towards the price of a commodity purchased.

7. Bai al Dayn

This is a short-term debt financing facility for commercial purposes by way of sale/purchase of trade documents.

8. Bai al Salam

Bai al Salam refers to advance payment for goods which are to be delivered at a later date.

9. Bai Bithaman Ajil

Bai Bithaman Ajil means sale of goods on a deferred payment basis.

10. Fatwah

This means a religious decree.

11. Fiqh

Fiqh means Islamic jurisprudence.

12. Gharar

Means uncertainty or contingency in a contract, which is a fundamental prohibition in Islamic finance.

13. Hawala

Hawala means bill of exchange, promissory note, cheque or draft.

14. Haram

Means unlawful.

15. Ijara

Ijara is a leasing agreement whereby the bank buys a merchandise for a customer and then leases it back.

16. Maysir

Gambling, one of three fundamental prohibitions in Islamic finance.

17. Mudaraba

An investment partnership, in which a bank provides the capital and the business is managed by the other party. The profit is shared in a pre-agreed ratio, while any loss is borne by the investor.

18. Mudarib

In a Mudaraba agreement, the person who is the entrepreneur is known as Mudarib.

19. Murabaha

Murabaha is a credit facility in which the bank buys an item for a customer and then sells it to the customer on a deferred basis.

20. Musharaka

Musharaka refers to a joint business partnership in which all partners share the profit according to a specific ratio, while any loss is shared according to the ratio of their capital contribution.

21. Rab-al-maal

The person who invests the capital in a mudaraba contract is called Rab-al-maal.

22. Riba

In Islamic finance, Riba refers to interest charged on loans or interest given on deposits. Religious practice forbids riba. Riba is an Arabic word that means "usury" or " unjust".

23. Shari'ah Board

The committee of Islamic scholars for guiding and supervising the implementation of Shari'ah compliant products.

24. Sukuk

Sukuk is the Arabic name for Shari'ah compliant bonds. Sukuk gives a direct asset **ownership**, while bonds in Western finance provide only indirect ownership.

25. Takaful

Takaful means Islamic insurance. In takaful the members are the insurers as well as the insured.

CHAPTER 24

Banking

BANKING

Banking is the business of accepting deposits from customers at certain interest rates and lending such money to customers by charging interest. The interest received on loans create profit for the bank and its customers. A bank is a financial institution licensed by the banking authority of a country to accept deposits and make loans. But the banks may also perform other financial services such as credit cards, business banking, wealth management and insurance. There are different types of banks in India that perform different functions to cater to the various sections of the society. There are **scheduled banks, commercial banks, private banks, public banks** and so on. The Reserve Bank of India, mainly known as **RBI**, is India's central bank and regulatory body for the Indian banking system. The Federal Reserve Bank is the central bank of the United States. Most banks in the United States are insured by the Federal Deposit Insurance Corporation (FDIC), The FDIC covers deposit accounts upto specified limits (currently $ 250,000 per depositor, per insured bank for each account ownership). Similarly in India each depositor in a bank is insured up to a maximum of INR 5,00,000 for principal and interest. Different countries have different policies/ limits for deposit protection. Other than banks, examples of financial institutions include credit unions, mortgage lenders, credit card companies, insurance companies and so on. The banking industry continues to be on the innovation path. The latest innovations are Digital banks, and Payment banks.

Banking Terminology is very wide. This chapter covers a list of commonly used terminologies.

1. Aadhaar Enabled Payment System (AEPS)

Aadhaar Enabled Payment System (AEPS) is a payment service that allows a bank customer to use Aadhaar as his/her identity to access his/her Aadhaar enabled bank account and perform basic banking transactions like balance enquiry, cash withdrawal, and remittances through a Business Correspondent. One has to be extremely careful in using such system as cyber crimes using this system is being noted.

2. Account Application

An application to be filled and signed by the customer for opening bank accounts. There are certain documents required by the bank at the time of submitting the account application.

3. Accrued Interest

Interest earned but not paid yet

4. American Bankers Association (ABA)

American Bankers Association (ABA), founded in 1875, is the largest banking trade association in the United States. The ABA represents small, regional and large banks. It offers a wide range of consultations in the field of staff training, insurance, capital management, asset management, and risk management.

5. Annual Percentage Rate (APR)

It is the cost of credit expressed as an annual rate in percentage terms. It is also the annual interest you earn on the money deposited into the bank account.

6. Annual Percentage Yield (APY)

A percentage rate for the total interest paid for a customer deposit based on the interest rate and the effect of compounding. For example, if you place a deposit for $100 at an interest rate of 4% for one year, you get $104.06 at the end of the year on a quarterly compounding basis. The APY in this case is 4.06%.

7. Annuity

A regular annual payment of money purchased by an immediate lumpsum amount paid in advance

8. Available for Sale (AFS)

Available for sale are securities held with the intention of selling it before maturity. These securities are valued at the fair value which is the available market price.

9. Bank Credit

Bank credit refers to lending by a bank, by means of bank advances, discounting bills, or purchasing securities.

10. Bank Custodian

A bank custodian is responsible for the safety of customers' assets held at the custodian's facility.

11. Banking Day

The day when bank is open for transactions at the branch.

12. Bank Deposits

Bank deposits are funds deposited by a customer in bank accounts.

13. Bank Note

A bank note is a type of negotiable promissory note, made by a bank, payable to the bearer on demand.

14. Bank Rate

A bank rate is the interest rate at which a nation's central bank lends money to domestic banks, often in the form of very short-term loans. Managing the bank rate is method by which central banks manage economic activity.

15. Bank Run

A bank run occurs when a large group of customers withdraw their savings and deposits at once fearing that the bank may go insolvent.

16. Bankrupt

A person or entity is bankrupt when their assets are insufficient to cover their debt.

17. Beneficiary

A person who is entitled to receive the benefits of a will, trust, annuity, pension plan, insurance policy or any other contract

18. Bearer cheque

A bearer cheque is the one which is payable to the person bearing or carrying that to the bank. It is transferable by delivery. You can identify a bearer cheque when you see the words "or bearer" printed on the cheque. A bearer cheque is payable by the bank without any further authorization by the issuer.

19. BHIM

BHIM is an Indian mobile payment app, developed by the National Payments Corporation of India, based on the Unified Payments Interface. The objective is to facilitate e-payments directly through banks and encourage cashless transactions.

20. Bill of Exchange

A Bill of Exchange is an instrument in writing, containing an unconditional order, signed by the banker, directing a certain person to pay a certain sum of money only to or to the order of a certain person or to the bearer of the instrument.

21. Bridge Loan

A short-term loan made by a bank to make up for temporary cash shortage

22. Bulk Deposit

A Bulk Deposit is a single deposit of Rupees two crores and above in Scheduled Commercial Banks and Small Finance Banks.

23. Callable FD

An FD that can be withdrawn prior to maturity

24. Call Money

Money loaned by a bank which is repayable on demand. A high portion of these funds are borrowed literally "at call" and hence the name.

25. Cash

Cash means money in the form of bank notes and coins.

26. Cashier's Cheque

A cheque drawn on the funds of the bank, and not on the funds in a depositor's account. However, the depositor has paid the funds to the bank in advance for issuing the cashier's cheque and hence the recipient of the cheque is assured of the funds.

27. Cash Deposit Machine (CDM)

It is an ATM like machine which allows you to deposit cash into your account directly using the ATM cum debit card. The advantage is that you need not go to a branch to deposit cash. Different banks may have different policies for deposit of cash through CDM. As per RBI guideline, a person can deposit upto Rs. 49,950 per day per account if his PAN is not updated with the bank. For depositing more than Rs.49,950, your PAN has to be updated with the bank. There are different rules regarding deposit of cash through CDM in foreign countries also.

28. Cash Reserve Ratio (CRR)

Cash Reserve Ratio means the liquid cash that banks have to maintain with the Reserve Bank of India as a certain percentage of their total deposits. This is an RBI requirement. The rate as of December 2023 was 4.5%. This means that with each Rs.100 deposits, the bank must maintain Rs. 4.50 as a reserve with RBI.

29. Central Bank Digital Currency (CBDC)

Central Bank Digital Currency (CBDC) is a digital form of currency issued by central banks of various countries. CBDCs are not cryptocurrencies, although the idea of CBDC stems from cryptocurrencies and block chain technology. Some central banks have already issued CBDCs. India has started the pilot CBDC on November 1, 2022. CBDCs are regulated by the respective central bank. CBDC exists only in digital form. Many requirements for physical currencies, such as minting facilities, are not required for digital currencies. Moreover, they are not subject to soiling or physical defects.

30. Certificate of Deposit (CD)

A document, which is issued by a bank acknowledging a deposit of money with the bank and constituting a promise to repay that sum, to the bearer, at a specified future date.

31. Cheque

A cheque is a document drawn on a bank, directing the bank to pay the sum specified in the cheque to the person whose name is borne on the cheque. For the bank to honour the cheque, there are certain terms and conditions to be met, for example there should be sufficient money in the account of the customer (drawer) to cover the cheque amount and the cheque amount should agree in both words and figures.

32. Cheque Fraud

Cheque frauds are of different types, such as altering cheque details, theft of cheque, counterfeiting of cheque, and depositing a cheque into an account other than the payee's account.

33. CIBIL Score

CIBIL Score is a three-digit numeric summary of your credit history. The score is derived using the credit history found in the CIBIL Report (also known as Credit Information Report or CIR). A CIR is an individual's credit payment history across loan types and credit institutions over a period of time. The rating ranges from 300 to 900. A rating closer to 900 means your credit rating is higher. CIBIL Score plays a critical role in the Loan Approval Process. Higher the

Score, higher are your chances of Loan Approval. TransUnion CIBIL Limited, an RBI approved credit information company operating in India maintains the CIBIL scores.

34. Commercial Banks

Commercial banks are those banks, which accept deposits and make payments, etc.

35. Compound Interest

Compound interest is the interest on interest. This can be illustrated using an example: if you have a fixed deposit for Rs.1,000 that earns 5% each year, and assuming that the bank compounds interest annually, you will have Rs.1,050 at the end of the first year. At the end of second year, you will have Rs.1,102.50. In fact, banks in India compound interest on FDs on a quarterly basis. The compounded interest is then reinvested with the principal amount. The maturity period of cumulative FDs ranges anywhere from six months to 10 years.

36. Consumer Credit

A loan given by a bank to its customer for a short period of time for the purchase of a specific commodity

37. Credit Card

A card issued by a bank to its customer, which provides the customer direct access to credit for merchant transactions. The credit card is a financial instrument that works on the concept of purchasing now and paying later. Thus a credit card offers the flexibility to make transactions on credit independent of the cardholder's account balance. The transaction limit, validity of the card and other terms are fixed by the bank issuing the card.

38. Credit Rating

Credit rating or credit report is an assessment of a borrower's creditworthiness in general terms. A credit rating is assigned to an entity, whether an individual, a corporation, a state or a sovereign government by a rating agency. In order to apply for a loan, issue a bond or seek a mortgage loan, a credit rating is a must. Such rating is usually issued, by a rating agency such as Standard and Poor's, Moody's or Fitch for a borrowing in the international debt market. CRISIL, ICRA, and CARE are some of Indian rating agencies.

39. Crossing of a Cheque

Crossing a cheque means drawing two parallel lines across the face of a cheque or at the top left-hand corner. Between the lines, two or more words such as ' and company' or ' not negotiable' or ' account payee' are written. A crossed cheque can't be cashed immediately by the holder over the bank counter, instead it has to be deposited directly to the account of the payee with the bank.

40. Truncation System (CTS)

Cheque Truncation System (CTS) is a process of clearing cheques electronically rather than processing the physical cheque by the presenting bank en-route to the paying bank. It is a step undertaken by the Reserve Bank of India for quicker cheque clearance.

41. Currency Code

The currency code is a three-letter alphabetic code representing a currency. The official currency codes are those issued by the International Standards Organization (ISO 4217) in 1978. In the foreign exchange market currencies are quoted using the currency codes. Following are some of the leading currency codes:

Australian Dollar	AUD
British Pound Sterling	GBP
Canadian Dollar	CAD
Chinese Renminbi	CNY
Euro	EUR
Indian Rupee	INR
Japanese Yen	JPY
Russian Ruble	RUB
Saudi Riyal	SAR
US Dollar	USD

The three letter alphabetic codes have also numeric three - digit codes.

42. Demand Draft

A demand draft is a negotiable instrument similar to a bill of exchange, issued by a bank to a customer, directing another bank or one of its own branches, to pay a certain sum of money to a party, who is specified in the instrument.

43. Debit Card

A debit card permits an account holder to access his funds electronically. When you use a debit card for a payment, the amount is immediately debited from your account. A debit card is used to obtain cash from an ATM or make a payment through point of sale system or pay for a purchase online.

44. Demonetization

Demonetization is the act of stripping a currency unit of its status as legal tender. It is implemented when there is a change in national currency. An existing currency is withdrawn from circulation and retired, by replacing with new notes or coins. A good example of demonetization is the demonetization of all Rs.500 and Rs.1,000 banknotes by Government of India and the issuance of new Rs.500 and Rs.2,000 banknotes in exchange for the demonetized banknotes. Rs.2,000 notes were also withdrawn in 2023.

45. Deposit Insurance and Credit Guarantee Corporation (DICGC)

Deposit Insurance and Credit Guarantee Corporation (DICGC) is a wholly-owned subsidiary of the Reserve Bank of India (RBI). It provides deposit insurance that works as a protection cover for bank deposit holders when the bank fails to pay its depositors. The agency insures all kinds of deposit accounts of a bank, such as savings, current, recurring, and fixed deposits upto a limit of Rs. 5 lakh per account holder per bank. The amount of Rs. 5 lakh includes principal and interest.

46. Deposit Slip

A deposit slip is a form that a customer has to fill with details of cash or cheque he deposits into his bank account.

47. Depositor Education and Awareness Fund (DEAF)

The Reserve Bank of India has mandated banks to identify accounts where there has been no customer-initiated transaction for a period of more than 10 years. As per the regulation, banks are required to transfer credit balance in such accounts to Depositors Education and Awareness Fund (DEAF). It is mandated for banks to show the details of unclaimed accounts on their official websites along with some identifiable details. Public sector banks transferred Rs 36,185 crores unclaimed deposits to Depositor Education and Awareness Fund till March 31, 2023.

48. Devaluation

Devaluation is the process of downward adjustment in the value of a country's currency. Devaluing a currency reduces the cost of a country's exports which in turn makes the exports attractive to international buyers.

49. Digital Bank

Digital Banks, otherwise DB banks, are full scale banks licensed under Banking Regulation Act. Unlike traditional banks which require physical presence (brick and mortar), digital banks deliver banking services through mobile applications and internet- based platforms. With digital accounts, account holders can manage their accounts digitally through smart phones. Digital banking is becoming the preferred banking medium among the new generation.

50. Digital Currency (Digital Money)

Digital currency refers to currency in digital or electronic form. It is also called Digital money. Digital money is not physically tangible like a dollar bill or Rupee note or a coin. The transactions in digital currency take place using online systems with the use of computers or mobile phones. Examples of digital currency are cryptocurrencies, central bank digital currencies and stablecoins. Digital currencies are the cheapest method of trading currencies as they do not require intermediaries. There are advantages and disadvantages with digital currencies. While cheaper transaction costs are the main advantages, they may be volatile to trade or subject to hacking.

51. Digital Rupee

Digital Rupee is one form of digital currency to be issued by India's Reserve Bank of India. India launched its pilot central bank digital currency on November 1, 2022. Initially nine banks would participate in the pilot programme, with a retail version of the digital Rupee to be issued later.

52. Dishonour of a Cheque

A payer is the one who issues a cheque to the payee. The payee deposits the cheque in his account in the bank. If the bank refuses to pay the amount mentioned on the cheque, the cheque is dishonoured. Cheques are dishonoured for various reasons. Cheques are dishonoured by the bank, if there are insufficient funds in the payer's account, if there is a signature mismatch, a mistake in the cheque, overwriting in the cheque, or if the cheque is not presented within the period stipulated by monetary authorities. As per the current guidelines of RBI, the validity period of a cheque is 3 months from the date of issue. A cheque after the 3 month period is called a stale cheque.

53. Documentation Fee

During the process of reviewing a lending application, the lender (bank) has to do a credit appraisal of the loan applicant. Customers will be charged for this service and the fee is called documentation fee.

54. Dovish Statement

This refers to a statement by the Federal Reserve suggesting that inflation effects are insignificant and there is unlikelihood that the bank may take aggressive measures.

55. Drawer of Cheque

Drawer of a cheque is the person who writes it.

56. Drawee

The person or the bank that is asked to make payment by the drawer.

57. eCheque

eCheque means an electronic cheque. It's a method of payment between two parties that mimics a cheque – only it's digital. It is a way to send money from a sender's account directly to the recipient. An eCheque contains the information that a paper cheque would. eCheques are governed by the same banking laws as paper cheques.

58. Electronic Banking

Electronic banking is a transaction that allows an account holder to obtain account information and manage transactions through a personal computer through the bank's website on internet. It is also called internet banking or online banking.

59. Electronic Funds Transfer (EFT)

Electronic Funds Transfer (EFT) refers to electronic transfer of funds between customers by electronic systems, such as ATMs, and electronic payments of bills without cash or cheques.

60. FATCA

FATCA means Foreign Account Tax Compliance Act. FATCA was enacted by US Congress in 2010 to target non-compliance by US tax payers using foreign bank accounts. FATCA requires US tax payers holding financial assets outside of the US to report such assets to the IRS on form no.8938. FATCA also requires certain foreign financial institutions to report directly to the IRS about financial accounts held by US Tax payers.

61. Federal Reserve System

Federal Reserve system is the central bank of the United States. The Fed, as it is called, regulates the monetary and financial system in USA.

62. Federal Funds (Fed Funds)

Federal Funds (Fed Funds) rate is the interest rate at which banks in the US borrow and lend overnight. The rate is set by the US Federal Reserve.

63. Federal Discount Rate

Federal discount rate is the rate set by the US Federal Reserve on loans extended to commercial banks and other depository institutions.

64. Fiat Money

Fiat money includes coins and paper money issued by a government which is the legal tender. It is not backed by any commodity such as gold or silver.

65. Fintech

Fintech literally means "financial technology". It includes all businesses in the banking and financial sector that use technology.

66. Fixed Deposit Laddering (FD Laddering)

FD laddering means dividing your investments in bank fixed deposits in different smaller amounts and different maturities to take advantage of rising interest rates. This strategy helps earn higher returns in a rising interest rate environment without penal interest rates when FDs have to be broken. This is also a recommended strategy to manage liquidity.

67. Foreclosure

Foreclosure is the legal process by which the collateral of a loan is sold to repay the loan, when the loan is in default.

68. Foreign Currency Non- Resident Account (FCNR)

Foreign Currency Non - Resident accounts (FCNR) are accounts maintained in India by Non-Residents in foreign currencies. Mostly the accounts are deposits in US Dollars and Pound Sterling.

69. GIFT City

Gujarat International Finance Tec-City (GIFT city) in Gandhinagar, Gujarat is a global financial and IT services hub, the first of its kind in India. State - of- the-art connectivity, infrastructure and transportation access have been integrated into the design of the city.

70. Hawkish Statement

This describes a statement from the Federal Reserve indicating that it may raise interest rates. The statement is called hawkish because it indicates the concern of Federal Reserve about rising inflation.

71. Held for Trading (HFT)

These are securities held for trading by taking advantage of short-term swings in the price due to interest rate changes.

72. Held to Maturity (HTM)

These are securities held with the intention of holding them until maturity.

73. Hotlisting a Card

Once a card is hotlisted, the bank blocks any transactions that will take place with the use of the card. In other words, any activity from that account will not be permitted. The card holder has to apply for a new card.

74. Hypothecation

Hypothecation is the process of pledging an asset as collateral for a loan, without giving up the title, possession or ownership rights. For example, you take a car loan from a bank and you agree to provide the car as collateral. The bank technically holds your car during the tenure of the loan, though you physically have the possession of it. If you don't pay the loan, the bank will repossess the car.

75. Identity Theft Fraud

Identity theft is the act of stealing a person's identity and using that identity to make financial gain. A bank account holder has to take several precautions to prevent such frauds, such as password security, website access precaution, disable auto log-in, and avoiding suspicious emails or phone calls.

76. Immediate Payment Service (IMPS)

IMPS provides a real time funds transfer service between banks in India through various channels such as mobile, internet, ATM and SMS. The maximum limit for a transfer is Rs.5 lakhs, although the limit can vary from bank to bank.

77. Indian Banks Association (IBA)

Indian Banks Association (IBA) is a representative body of banks operating in India with the objective of promoting and developing sound banking principles, conventions, and practices. The members of IBA include public sector banks, private sector banks, co-operative sector banks, rural banks, foreign banks operating in India and financial institutions. It is head quartered in Mumbai and has 237 members.

78. Indian Institute of Banking and Finance (IIBF)

Indian Institute of Banking and Finance (IIBF), formerly known as Indian Institute of Bankers (IIB), is a national apex body owned by the Ministry of Finance, Government of India, with the objective of providing professional education in banking and finance. The institute conducts certification for three flagship courses, diploma level courses, certification courses, blended courses and advanced management programmes.

79. Individual Retirement Accounts (IRA)

Individual Retirement Account is a retirement savings account in the US to which yearly tax-deductible contributions upto a certain limit are made. The amount contributed is not taxed until withdrawn. Withdrawal without penalty is not permitted until the individual reaches the age of 59 ½.

80. International Financial Services Centre Authority (IFSCA)

IFSCA, headquartered in GIFT city, Gandhinagar, Gujarat is a unified authority for the development and regulation of financial products, financial services, and financial institutions in the international financial services centre (IFSC) in India.

81. Internet Banking

Internet Banking, or net banking, or online banking, is an electronic payment system that enables a customer to do a range of financial transactions through the website of a bank.

82. Insolvent

A person is insolvent when he is unable to meet his debts as they become due in the normal course of business.

83. Institute of Banking Personnel Selection (IBPS)

Institute of Banking Personnel Selection (IBPS) is a central recruiting agency in India, owned by the Ministry of Finance of the government, with the aim of recruiting and placing personnel in various nationalized banks and rural banks.

84. Interest

Interest is the payment a borrower pays the lender for the use of money for a period of time. In other words it is the cost of borrowing money, expressed as a percentage. Interest can be either simple interest or compound interest.

85. Lease Agreement

Lease agreement is a legal contract between a lessor and lessee that allows the lessee to use an asset owned by the lessor for a period of time at an agreed fee for the lease term. Typically lease agreements are used for rental properties, but they are also used for rental of vehicles, construction equipments and household appliances.

86. Letter of Credit (LC or LOC)

A letter of credit is a guarantee by the bank to pay the buyer's payment to the seller. The bank ensures full and timely payment to the seller. The bank charges a fee for issuing the LC.

87. Letter of Hypothecation

A letter of hypothecation is an authorization letter given to the bank by an exporter to sell the goods exported, in case the importer fails to make payment for the goods imported and remit the proceeds less expenses to the exporter.

88. Lien

Lien is a claim against a property or an asset. It is the right of possession of an asset owned by a person until the debt owed by that person is discharged. For example, some banks note a lien on FDs held by a customer against the issue of credit card to the customer.

89. Ink Character Recognition (MICR)

MICR (magnetic ink character recognition) is a technology used to verify the legitimacy of cheques through certain characters on the cheques. There is a nine-digit number at the bottom left side of a cheque, which is the routing code of the bank on which the cheque is drawn and it is printed in magnetic ink.

90. Maturity

Maturity is the date on which the principal balance of a loan, bond, deposit or any financial instrument becomes due and payable.

91. Mezzanine Debt

Mezzanine debt bridges the gap between debt and equity financing. It is one of the highest- risk forms of debt as it is subordinate to pure debt but senior to pure equity.

92. Microfinance

Microfinance is a type of banking service extended to unemployed or low income group, who are typically excluded from traditional banking. Microfinance institutions extend credit as working capital loans to low income group. Examples of low income group are basket weavers, self employed tailors, etc.

93. Mobile Banking

Mobile banking is the act of doing financial transactions through a mobile device (cell phone or tablet). Mobile banking is very convenient in today's digital world. But there are disadvantages also, such as the limitations on the type of transactions that can be done physically at a bank and security concerns.

94. Money Transfer – Key Terms

94.1. Automated Clearing House (ACH)

An ACH is an electronic fund transfer made between banks and credit unions across what is called the Automated Clearing House network.

94.2. Cash Pickup

Cash pickup is a money transfer retrieval option offered through some providers that allows the recipient of the money transfer to collect cash from a physical location nearby rather than receiving the money through a bank account.

94.3. eChecks

An eCheck is an electronic check payment that uses ACH to direct debit from one bank account to another.

94.4. Exchange Rate

An exchange rate is the rate at which one country's currency is converted into another. In other words, an exchange rate is the price of a country's currency in terms of another currency. Exchange rates fluctuate daily due to market forces and other factors.

94.5. Forex

Forex stands for Foreign Exchange, which means trading one currency for another.

94.6. IBAN

An IBAN, or International Bank Account Number, is a number used to identify an overseas bank account. An IBAN is used when sending money between banks, typically internationally. The IBAN number consists of a two-letter country code, followed by two check digits, and up to thirty-five alphanumeric characters. These alphanumeric characters are known as the basic bank account number (BBAN).

94.7. Mobile Wallet

A mobile wallet is a digital wallet that stores your payment information on a mobile device. Most mobile wallets allow you to enter your credit card information for easy purchasing.

94.8. MT103. Document

A MT103 document acts as a confirmation of payment made from your bank when you complete an international money transfer. It includes the beneficiary's information along with all other important details of the transaction.

94.9. MTCN

MTCN is a 10-digit Money Transfer Control Number you may receive when sending money in order to track your transaction. The recipient will also receive the same MTCN, and will need this number to retrieve the funds.

94.10. Routing Number

Routing numbers are nine-digit numbers that identify your bank or credit union in a financial transaction, and are used by banks to direct the exchange of funds to and from accounts.

94.11. SWIFT

SWIFT stands for Society of Worldwide Interbank Financial Telecommunication. It represents a global messaging network that banks and financial institutions use to securely and efficiently send and receive information, including pertaining to money transfers.

94.12. SWIFT Code

A SWIFT code is a string of 8 or 11 characters assigned to every bank that belongs to the SWIFT network. SWIFT codes identify bank branches for international transactions to ensure quick and accurate fund transfers. The code identifies the individual bank and its location, acting as a form of an international bank ID. Each bank has a unique SWIFT code. It usually consists of 11 characters divided into four groups: first, four letters to identify the bank; second, two letters to identify the country; third, two letters to indicate the bank's location; and fourth (which is optional), three digits to specify the receiving branch.

94.13. Wire transfer

The term "wire transfer" is often used to refer to any electronic transfer of money from one person to another.

95. Monthly Average Balance (MAB)

Monthly Average Balance (MAB) is the minimum balance an account should have on an average at any point in the month. MAB requirement varies from bank to bank. Penalty may be applicable if MAB is not maintained.

96. NABARD

National Bank for Agriculture and Rural Development (NABARD), established in 1982 by an Act of the Parliament as a development bank of the nation for the prosperity of rural India. It is mandated for providing and regulating credit facilities for small scale industries, cottage and village industries, handicrafts and rural crafts, and other economic activities in rural India.

97. National Automated Clearing House (NACH)

NACH is a funds clearing platform set up by the National Payments Corporation of India, similar to the ECS of RBI.

98. National Electronic Funds Transfer (NEFT)

The National Electronic Funds Transfer (NEFT) system is a nation-wide electronic funds transfer system to transfer funds from one bank account to another in a safe manner. To initiate a NEFT transfer, the payee name, bank account, bank branch details and the IFSC code of the bank are required. The NEFT settlements are made on a batch system.

99. National Payment Corporation of India (NPCI)

National Payment Corporation of India (NPCI) is an initiative of Reserve Bank of India (RBI) and Indian Banks Association (IBA) under the provisions of the Payments and Settlements Act 2007, to ensure a robust payments and settlements infrastructure in India. It facilitates services like UPI Payment, Rupay, Bharat Bill Pay, NACH, FASTag, IMPS, CTS, BHIM Aadhaar Pay, and other payment platforms.

100. Nationalized Banks in India

Nationalized banks in India are banks owned by the Government of India. They are also known as public sector banks. As of 2024, there are 12 nationalized banks in India. They are Bank of Baroda, Bank of India, Bank of Maharashtra, Canara Bank, Central Bank of India, Indian Bank, Indian Overseas Bank, Punjab National Bank, Punjab and Sind Bank, State Bank of India, UCO Bank, and Union Bank of India. State Bank of India was the first bank to be nationalized. It was on July 19, 1969 the then Prime Minister Indira Gandhi nationalized 14 banks in India. The other banks were nationalized during 1969 to 1981. After massive merger, the number of nationalized banks was reduced to 12 from 27 banks in 2017.

101. Negotiable Instrument

A negotiable instrument is a document guaranteeing the payment of money stated in the document upon demand or at a set time.

The name of the payee will be listed on the document. Examples of negotiable instruments are cheques, drafts, bills of exchange, etc.

102. Negotiable Instruments Act, 1881

All negotiable instruments in India are governed by the Negotiable Instruments Act 1881, an act prevailing in India from the time of the British Colonial rule, which remains largely unchanged.

103. No-Frills Account

This is a savings account which doesn't require a minimum balance to enjoy the benefits like net banking, online funds transfer, etc.

104. Non-Callable FD

In a non-callable FD, the depositor cannot withdraw the deposit prior to maturity.

105. Note Sorting Machine (NSM)

A machinery for automatic counting, sorting and fitness checking of currency notes.

106. One Time Password (OTP)

OTP is a SMS system in banking that sends a one time password to the customer's mobile or email registered with the bank to log into internet banking or to approve transactions online. It is a four to six digit code that pops up on the mobile or in the email system whenever a debit/credit card is used for an online transaction or to log into the system for internet banking.

107. Order Cheque

An order cheque is a cheque on which the words "or bearer" is cancelled or " or order" is printed. Such cheques are payable to the person whose name appears on the cheque. Bank may verify the identity of the person before making payment.

108. Outstanding Cheque

An outstanding cheque is a cheque issued by an account holder but not yet presented for payment or paid by the account holder's bank.

109. Overdraft

Overdraft is a form of bank lending, by which an account holder is permitted to draw cheques beyond the credit balance in his account. Interest at a set rate is payable on the overdrawn amount.

110. Passbook

It is a book issued to the customers by a bank showing the account details, some basic information about the account holder such as address and contact number and some details about the bank branch where the account is maintained. The photograph of the account holder is also affixed on the first page of the passbook. All deposits and withdrawal are entered in the passbook. In other words, a passbook is a copy of the account holder's ledger in the bank's books. Passbook is also an Officially Valid Document for address proof in the KYC process.

111. Payment Aggregator

A payment aggregator is a payment service provider through which e-commerce merchants can process their payment transactions. An aggregator allows merchants to accept different payment instruments such as credit card, bank transfers,e-money without having to set up merchant accounts with a bank or credit card association. The aggregator provides the means for facilitating payment from the consumer to the merchant. In January 2023 RBI gave in principle approval to BharatPe to operate as a Payment Aggregator.

112. Payment Bank

Payment banks are new model of banks conceptualized by Reserve Bank of India. A payment bank is like any other bank, operating on a smaller scale without any credit risk. In simple terms a payment bank can carry out most banking services but can't advance loans or issue credit cards. It can accept deposits (upto INR 2 lakh currently), offer remittance services, provide ATM services/debit cards, net banking and third party fund transfers. Airtel Payment Bank was the first payment bank licensed in India in 2016. It is not mandatory to open a minimum of 25% branches in unbranched rural area, but it is required to have a minimum of 25% physical access points in rural areas. The banking access points can be post offices, petrol stations, merchant outlets and even small shops.

113. Peer to Peer (P2P) Lending

This refers to an online platform that matches borrowers and lenders.

114. Personal Identification Number (PIN)

The PIN is a secret code given by a bank to debit or credit cardholders to access their accounts. It is generally a four number code. It is randomly issued by the bank or selected by the cardholder. The purpose is to prevent the unauthorized use of the card.

115. Phishing

Phishing is the act of defrauding online a customer of financial information by posing as a legitimate entity such as banker, insurance agent, or a government official. These fraudsters pressurize customers into urgently sharing their confidential details, citing some emergency situations.

116. Plastic Money

Plastic money refers to Debit and Credit cards, where hard cash is not used. Plastic money is also called E-money.

117. Politically Exposed Person (PEP)

Politically exposed persons are Individuals who are or have been entrusted with prominent public functions in a foreign country eg: Heads of States or Governments, Senior Politicians, Senior government/ Judiciary/ Military officers, senior executives of state owned corporations, important political party officials etc.

118. Positive Pay System (PPS)

In 2020, RBI has issued a notification introducing Positive Pay System for cheque truncation. The concept of PPS involves a process of confirming certain key details of a cheque issued by the drawer to the drawee bank. Under this process, the drawee informs the drawee bank, electronically (SMS, email, mobile app, ATM etc.) certain minimum details of the cheque (date of issue, name of payee, amount.), which will then be cross checked with the cheque presented for payment by CTS. In case of any discrepancy, CTS will flag it to the drawee and presenting bank, who would take redressal measures. The system is applicable for cheques with INR 50,000 and above. While availing of this facility is at the discretion of the account holder, banks are making it mandatory for cheques with INR 5,00,000 and above.

119. Prime Lending Rate (PLR)

Prime Lending Rate refers to the interest rate charged by US banks to their reputed and creditworthy customers on short term loans. In India the Benchmark Prime Lending Rate or **BPLR** was introduced in 2003 by RBI. It is the rate charged by a commercial bank to its most creditworthy customers.

120. PSU Banks in India

Public Sector Undertakings (Banks) are a major type of government owned banks in India, where the Ministry of finance of the government of India or the Ministry of Finance of a state government holds majority stake (i.e,50% or more). Such banks are listed on the stock exchanges in India. They are also known as Public Sector Banks (PSBs).

121. Remote Access Applications Fraud

In this type of fraud, fraudsters ask the victims to download sharing applications and then ask the victims to share a code which then gives them access to victim's mobile, laptop or desktop. With OTPs received on the compromised device, the fraudsters carry out unauthorized transactions in the victim's account.

122. Repo Rate

Repo rate is the rate at which the central bank of a country lends money to commercial banks when there is a shortage of funds in the system. Repo rate is used by central banks to manage liquidity and in turn control inflation. In India also Reserve Bank of India uses Repo rate to manage liquidity and regulate interest rate to control inflation.

123. Reverse Repo Rate

Reverse repo rate is the rate at which RBI borrows money from commercial banks for short term. It is an important tool used by RBI to manage liquidity and inflation. Reverse repo rate is lower than the Repo rate.

124. Revolving Credit Facility

Revolving credit is a facility extended by banks, that is renewed as existing loan is repaid and the facility continues. Credit card is one form of revolving credit.

125. Resident Foreign Currency Account (RFC)

Resident Foreign Currency accounts (RFC) are bank accounts maintained by residents in foreign currency. Only NRIs who have returned to India can maintain RFC accounts. RFC accounts can be savings, current or foreign currency deposit accounts. This type of account is to assist NRIs who have returned to India and who want to keep their foreign currency in India. However, there are rules applicable for maintaining such accounts.

126. Rupay

Rupay is an Indian multinational financial services and payment services system launched by the National Payments Corporation of India in 2012. It was created to fulfill RBI's vision of launching a domestic, open, and multilateral payment system. It is India's first-of-its-kind domestic debit card payment network.

127. Rupee Symbol

The symbol of the Indian Rupee is "₹". The design resembles both the Devanagiri letter "₹" (ra) and the Latin capital letter " R" with a double horizontal line at the top. The new sign was adopted by Government of India on 15th July 2010. It was designed by D.Udaya Kumar. The currency code (ISO 4217) of Indian Rupee is **INR.**

128. Securitization

Securitization is the process of converting a bank loan into a marketable and negotiable security.

129. Senior Citizen

An individual resident who is 60 years and above in age but less than 80 years is considered as Senior Citizen in India. A Super Senior Citizen is an individual resident who is 80 years or above.

130. Signature Card

Signature card is a card signed by the customer showing his specimen signature, which is used by the bank as an identification.

131. Skimming

In this type of fraud, fraudsters install skimming devices in ATM machines to copy data from your debit/credit cards. PIN is captured by installing a dummy keypad or a camera.

132. Simple Interest

Simple interest is an easy method of calculating the interest on a loan for a period. It is calculated by multiplying the principal amount by the daily interest rate by the days for which the borrowed money is used. To understand how simple interest rate works, assume you have a car loan of Rs. 100,000 at a simple interest rate of 7.3% per annum, and you pay the interest monthly, then your interest for the month (assuming 30 days for the month and 365 days for an year) will be: 100,000 x 7.3 /100 / 365 x 30 = **600**. The interest for the month is Rs.600.

133. Smishing

Smishing means SMS plus Phishing. It is a type of social engineering fraud in which a target customer is contacted through SMS and lured into divulging their sensitive information.

134. Stale Cheque

A cheque, if not presented within the validity period, becomes a stale cheque. Each country has validity period for cheques. Currently a three months period from the issue date is the validity period of a cheque in India and after that period the cheque becomes a stale cheque and will not be paid by the bank.

135. Statutory Liquidity Ratio (SLR)

Statutory Liquidity Ratio (SLR) is the minimum percentage of deposit a commercial bank has to maintain, either in the form of cash, gold or any other security. In other words, it is the basic reserve requirement that a bank has to maintain before extending credit to customers.

136. Stop Payment

The act of stopping the payment of a cheque issued but not presented yet for payment.

137. Sub Prime Borrowers

Subprime borrowers are those with a history of loan default, those with a history of bankruptcy, and those with low income relative to their mortgage payment ability.

138. Sub Prime Loans

Subprime loans are loans extended to subprime borrowers.

139. Sub Prime Crisis

Subprime crisis is the crisis in the financial services that started in the United States in 2008 following a collapse in the home prices after the bubble in housing market. The subprime crisis developed into a global financial crisis.

140. Sustainability Linked Bonds

This is a new kind of bond with features based on whether the issuer (borrower) achieves sustainability goals by a deadline. Such bonds encourage the borrower to achieve sustainability targets within a set timeframe.

141. Sweep Facility

Sweep facility is a facility extended by banks to their customers whereby credit balances in the accounts are shifted to deposits which earn interest.

142. SWIFT CODE

SWIFT means the Society for Worldwide Interbank Financial Telecommunication. The system is used as a standardized and secure way of transferring international payments. SWIFT is essentially a messaging network to send and receive electronic information between banks. The SWIFT code contains 8 characters and banks use them to identify themselves globally.

143. Tokenization

Tokenization refers to the replacement of actual card (debit card/credit card) data for an alternate code called 'token'. Reserve Bank of India (RBI) has introduced tokenization for credit and debit cards in 2022. RBI is the first in the world to introduce 'tokenization'. The token is unique for a combination of the card, the token requestor (usually, the merchant), and the device. A card holder can request for tokenization through the merchant when using the card for an online purchase and the card network issues the token with the approval of the card issuer. Tokenization is intended for the safety of the card. A card which is tokenized can be de-tokenized later.

144. Unclaimed Deposits Gateway to Access Information (UDGAM)

UDGAM is a portal (**udgam.rbi.org.in**) initiated by RBI that allows individuals to search for unclaimed deposits across various banks in one convenient location.

145. UPI

Unified Payments Interface (UPI) is a payment system introduced by the National Payment Corporation of India (NPCI) in 2016 that allows customers to make instant transfer of money between banks.

146. Usury

The act of charging illegally high interest rate on a loan

147. Value Date

Value date refers to the date when a transaction takes place or when the value of assets or money becomes effective. In banking, value date typically refers to the date on which account holder can use funds from deposited checks.

148. Vishing

Vishing means voice plus phishing. It is a type of social engineering fraud in which a target customer is contacted through phone call and lure the customer to divulge his sensitive information.

149. Wire Transfer

The transfer of funds from one point to another by wire or network

CHAPTER 25

Central Banks

CENTRAL BANK

The Central Bank is an institution that manages the currency and monetary policy of a country or a formal monetary union and oversees their commercial banking system. The main objective of a central bank is price stability by setting the monetary policy and setting interest rates.

Following are the names of select central banks:

Country	Central Bank
China	People's Bank of China (PBoC)
European Union (19 countries)	European Central Bank (ECB)
India	Reserve Bank of India (RBI)
Japan	Bank of Japan (BOJ)
Russia	Bank of Russia (Central Bank of Russia-CBR)
United Kingdom	Bank of England (BOE)
United States	Federal Reserve Bank (FRB or Fed)

Frequently Used Jargons of Reserve Bank of India and Other Central Banks

1. Asset - Liability Management (ALM)

Asset Liability Management (ALM) is the process of managing the use of assets and cashflows to reduce the risk of loss from not paying liability on time. The process must ensure that assets are available to meet liability when they are due and that assets must be able to be converted into cash. ALM strives to avoid a mismatch between assets and liabilities.

2. Asset Liability Management Committee (ALCO)

ALCO is a strategic decision making body of a bank to oversee its asset liability management (ALM).

3. Asset Reconstruction Company (ARC)

An Asset Reconstruction Company (ARC) is a specialized financial institution that buys non-performing assets (NPAs) and other bad debts from banks and other financial institutions so that the latter can clean up their balance sheets. ARCs are regulated by RBI.

4. Banking Ombudsman

Banking ombudsman is a senior official appointed by Reserve Bank of India to attend to and resolve complaints of customers against banking services. He has a quasi-judicial authority in his functions.

5. Basel

Basel, also known as Basle, is a city in northwestern Switzerland on the river Rhine. The place is famous as a location for international meetings and exhibitions. Basel is also important for world banking. UBS AG maintains its central offices in Basel. The Bank for International Settlements (BIS) is located within the city. The Basel is also the location of the Basel committee for Banking supervision. It usually meets at the premises of BIS in Basel. The place is famous for the Basel accords (Basel I, Basel II and Basel III).

6. BASEL Capital Accord

The BASEL Capital Accord is an Agreement concluded among country representatives in 1988 to develop standardised risk-based capital requirements for banks across countries. The Accord was replaced with a new capital adequacy framework (BASEL II), published in June 2004. The latest accord BASEL III was agreed upon in November 2010, following the financial crisis.

7. BASEL Committee on Banking Supervision (BCBS)

The BASEL Committee is a committee of bank supervisors consisting of members from each of the G10 countries. The Committee is a forum for discussion about the supervisory problems among national authorities. This committee changed the Risk Management process in the banking industry.

8. BASEL III

Basel III is an internationally agreed set of measures developed by the Basel Committee on Banking Supervision in response to the financial crisis of 2007-09. The measures aim to strengthen the regulation, supervision and risk management of banks.

9. Basis Point

Basis point is one hundredth of one percent. One basis point is 0.01%. it is used for measuring change in interest rate or yield.

10. Capital Reserves

Capital reserves refer to a company's profits not paid out as dividends to shareholders, but ploughed back into business.

11. Capital to Risk Weighted Asset Ratio (CRAR)

CRAR shows the relationship between the capital and the risk weighted assets of a bank. It is calculated by dividing the capital of the bank with aggregated risk weighted assets for credit risk, market risk and operational risk. The higher the ratio, the better the bank is capitalized.

12. CASA

Deposit in bank in current and savings account.

13. Cash Reserve Ratio (CRR)

Cash Reserve Ratio (CRR) is the ratio of cash parked by commercial banks in their specified current accounts with RBI. CRR is fixed by RBI and is used as a tool for monetary policy control.

14. Credit Risk

Credit Risk is the risk of loss resulting from a borrower's inability to repay a loan. It refers to the risk that a lender may not get the principal and interest owed by a borrower.

15. Derivative Instruments

A derivative security is one that derives its value from the underlying asset. The three main types of derivatives are options, forward contracts and swaps.

16. Doubtful Asset

A doubtful asset is a substandard asset, which has remained in that category for 12 months.

17. Duration of a bond

Duration of a bond refers to a bond's interest rate risk that considers a bond's maturity, yield, coupon, and call features.

18. Federal Open Market Committee (FOMC)

Federal open market committee is a branch of the Federal Reserve System, that sets monetary policy and manages interest rates through open market operations.

19. Financial Engineering

Financial engineering is the use of mathematical techniques to solve financial problems, by using computer science, statistics, economics, and applied mathematics.

20. Financial Risk Manager (FRM)

Financial Risk Manager (FRM) is a professional designation issued by the Global Association of Risk Professionals (GARP). FRMs are specialized in assessing risk and managing risk. It typically applies for banks, insurance companies, regulatory agencies, accounting firms, and asset management companies.

21. Hybrid Debt Capital Instruments

Hybrid debt capital instruments incorporate the characteristics of equity and debt securities. The decision where such securities can be included in the Tier II capital of a bank depends on the features of supporting losses on an ongoing basis.

22. Integrated Ombudsman Scheme of RBI

A scheme for resolving grievances about the services provided by entities regulated by Reserve Bank of India in a cost effective and expeditious manner. A regulated entity means a bank, a Non-Banking Finance Company, a System Participant as defined in the scheme, or any entity as decided by RBI. This is the single point contact for all complaints with the aim of faster redressal of the complaints

23. Leverage

Leverage refers to the amount of debt a firm uses to finance assets.

24. Liquid Assets

Liquid assets of a bank consist of: cash, balances with RBI, balances in current accounts with banks, money at call and short notice, inter-bank placements due within 30 days and securities under "held for trading" and "available for sale" categories excluding securities that do not have ready market.

25. London Interbank Rate (LIBOR)

LIBOR is the interest rate at which banks offer to lend among themselves in the interbank market in London. It is calculated as an average of the indications received from banks in London. It is a key global benchmark for borrowing costs between banks.

26. Market Risk

Market risk is the risk for an investor due to various factors that affect the performance of the financial markets.

27. MIBOR

The Mumbai Interbank Offer Rate (MIBOR) is the rate of interest charged by a bank on a short-term loan to another bank. MIBOR is used in conjunction with the Mumbai interbank bid and forward rates (**MIBID** and **MIFOR**) by RBI to set short-term monetary policy.

28. Modified Duration

Modified duration is a measure of the percentage change in the price of a bond for 1% change in yield.

29. Monetary Policy Committee (RBI)

The Monetary Policy Committee of RBI is responsible for fixing the benchmark interest rate in India. The meetings of the Monetary Policy Committee are held at least four times a year (at least once a quarter) and it publishes its decisions after each such meeting.

30. Policy Committee (UK)

The Monetary Policy Committee is a committee of the Bank of England, which meets for three and a half days, eight times a year, to decide the official interest rate in the United Kingdom.

31. Non-Performing Assets (NPA)

An asset on the bank's book becomes non-performing when the asset stops generating income for the bank.

32. Off Balance Sheet Exposure

Off Balance sheet exposure is an activity that does not reflect on the balance sheet of a bank. It generates fee income, but produce liabilities or assets contingent upon an event.

33. Official Discount Rate (ODR)

Official discount rate, also called bank rate, is the interest rate charged by a central bank on short-term loans to commercial banks and other financial intermediaries.

34. Operational Risk

Operational risk refers to the risk a bank might incur as a result of operational issues such as people risk, process risk, systems risk and events risk.

35. Quantitative Easing (QE)

Quantitative Easing (QE) is a form of monetary policy in which a central bank buys bonds from the open market to reduce interest rates and to increase money supply. As a result banks will have more liquidity to extend loans.

36. Quantitative Tightening (QT)

Quantitative Tightening (QT) is a form of monetary policy tightening by a central bank by selling bonds in the financial market to raise interest rates and reduce the liquidity in the economy. Banks will have less liquidity in this situation and hence interest rates will go up.

37. Revaluation Reserves

Revaluation reserves refer to reserves arising out of the revaluation of undervalued assets that are on the books of a bank, namely buildings, properties and financial securities.

38. Risk Weighted Asset (RWA)

Risk-weighted assets are used to determine the minimum capital requirements of banks, by assigning certain risk weights to each type of assets based on their riskiness. The more risk a bank is taking, the more capital is needed to protect the investors. For example, holding of Government bonds are less risky than the holdings of corporate bonds. Risk weighting of assets is a method to find the Capital Adequacy Ratio for a bank.

39. Statutory Liquidity Ratio (SLR)

Statutory Liquidity Ratio or SLR is a minimum percentage of deposits that a commercial bank has to maintain in the form of liquid cash, gold or other securities. It is basically the reserve requirement that banks are expected to keep before offering credit to customers. SLR is fixed by RBI and is used as a tool for monetary control.

40. Stress Testing

Stress test is an exercise to determine the vulnerability of a bank to an unlikely event with reference to its profitability or capital adequacy.

41. Subordinated Debt

Subordinated debt is a debt that is subordinated to all other debt. This means that in the event of a bankruptcy, subordinated debt holders will be paid only after all other debt holders are paid.

42. Substandard Assets

A substandard asset is an asset which has been an NPA for a period less than or equal to 12 months.

43. Targeted Longer-Term Refinancing Operations (TLTROs)

Targeted Longer-Term Refinancing Operations (TLTROs) is a tool used by Euro-system in its monetary operations. TLTROs is a non-regular, longer-term lending that the Euro-system extends to banks. The Euro-system includes the European Central Bank (ECB) and the Eurozone member central banks. Through TLTROs, the ECB offers longer-term loans to banks at favourable costs and encourages them to lend to businesses and consumers in the euro area. This keeps borrowing costs low and supports spending and investments.

44. Tier I Capital

Tier I capital refers to one of the components of regulatory capital for banks. It consists mainly of share capital and reserves (excluding goodwill). It is an indication of the bank's ability to absorb losses from its activities. Tier I capital is also known as "core capital".

45. Tier II Capital

Tier II capital refers to one of the components of regulatory capital for banks. It consists of certain reserves and certain subordinated debt. It is an indication of the bank's ability to absorb losses from its activities. It is also known as "supplementary capital". The loss absorption capacity of Tier II capital is less than that of Tier I capital.

46. Value at Risk (VaR)

VaR is defined as the estimate of loss in an asset/liability position during a given period at a given confidence level.

CHAPTER 26

Economics

1. Arbitrage Pricing Theory (APT)

Arbitrage Pricing Theory (APT) is a multi-factor asset pricing model based on the proposition that the expected return of an asset depends on several economic variables. As per APT, if the value of an asset happens to diverge from the theoretical price, arbitrage by investors should bring it back into line.

2. Balanced Budget

A government budget in which revenues perfectly offset expenditures so that there is neither a deficit nor a surplus.

3. Balance of Payment (BOP)

Balance of Payment is the difference between all the money entering and exiting a country during a given period.

4. Balance of Trade (BOT)

Balance of Trade is the difference between the exports and imports of a country during a set period.

5. Barter

Barter is a form of trade in which one good or service is exchanged for another, without the use of money as intermediary.

6. Bear Market

Bear market is the term used to represent the pessimism in the stock market, when prices of stocks undergo a prolonged decline.

7. Bull Market

Bull market is the term used to represent the optimism in the stock market, when stock prices are rising or expected to continue rising.

8. Business Cycle

Business cycle refers to a series of stages in an economy, as it expands and contracts. It is also referred as a 'trade cycle' or an 'economic cycle'.

9. Capacity Utilization

The capacity utilization rate indicates the capacity used in the production and is an indication of the growth of the economy.

10. Capital Asset Pricing Model (CAPM)

Capital Asset Pricing Model (CAPM) is a mathematical model that estimates the expected return of an investment, based on its riskiness relative to the market. The model establishes the required rate of return of an investment and its risk.

11. Capital Expenditure (CapEx)

Capital expenditure (CapEx) is the money that a company spends to acquire, update, or improve a fixed asset, such as a building, plant, or machinery. This type of financial outlay is made by companies to add some economic benefit to its operation.

12. Capital Flight

Capital flight refers to the withdrawal of financial capital from a country by investors due to non-favorable economic changes, political developments or any other factor.

13. Capitalism

An economic system in which privately owned companies and businesses undertake most of the economic activity.

14. Carbon Tax

Carbon Tax is an environmental tax imposed on products which use carbon based materials and cause greenhouse gas pollution.

15. Climate Change

The concentration of carbon dioxide and other gases in the atmosphere is increasing and absorbing solar energy, which results in the rise of average global temperatures.

16. Consumer Price Index (CPI)

Consumer Price Index (CPI) is a measure of the overall price level paid by consumers for the goods and services they purchase. Periodic change in the CPI index is a good measure of the consumer price inflation.

17. Consumption

Consumption refers to the goods and services which are used for their ultimate end. Consumption includes both private and public consumption.

18. Contagion

The transmission of an economic shock from one country to another

19. Credit Squeeze

Credit squeeze refers to the refusal of banks to give loans or extend credit to individuals and businesses because they are worried about the risk of default by borrowers. This is common in times of a recession or financial instability. Credit squeeze pushes down economic activity and affects job growth.

20. Currency in Circulation (CIC)

In monetary economics currency in circulation in a country refers to the value of currency and cash (bank notes and coins) issued by the central bank minus the amount that has been removed from the system. Currency in circulation is an important part of the money supply in a country. There are mainly three types of money in circulation: physical money (cash and coins), central bank reserves used by banks to make payment between themselves, and commercial bank money (various type of bank deposits, bank liabilities, and bank credit).

21. Deficit

When a government, or an individual spends more on consumption than the revenue they generate during a given period, they incur a deficit. A deficit has to be financed with new borrowings or using existing savings.

22. Deflation

Deflation is the general level of decline in prices for goods and services. Deflation occurs when inflation falls below 0%. Deflation reduces the value of a currency over time. It is also known as negative inflation. As deflation occurs, the purchasing power of money goes up, meaning you can buy more goods today for a Rupee, compared to what you could buy yesterday.

23. Depression

A depression is a very deep, long and painful recession in which output remains bleak and unemployment rises very sharply.

24. Discretionary Fiscal Policy

Discretionary fiscal policy means adjustment by a government in its taxing and spending policies due to changing economic situations.

25. Effective Exchange Rate

The effective exchange rate is a measure of one currency against a basket of other currencies. The effective exchange rate is good for looking at the overall performance of a currency. If the overall effective exchange rate of a currency increases, it means that currency is becoming stronger.

26. Employment Rate

Employment rate is a better measure of labour market, which is measured by the number of working age adults employed in paying positions.

27. Euro area

Euro area refers to the group of countries that have officially adopted Euro (€) as their currency.

28. Exchange Rate

Exchange rate is the price at which the currency of one country is exchanged for the currency of another country. A currency is strong when it can purchase more of the goods from another country. A currency is weak when it purchases less goods from another country. Fluctuations in the exchange rate of a country result in various economic implications.

29. Exports

Exports is the sale of products from one country to a purchaser in another country.

30. Four Percent Rule for Retirement Spending

In the US, the traditional advice for retirees who need to make their money last for 30 years of retirement is to spend no more than 4% of their savings in the first year of retirement, and in subsequent years raise those withdrawals to keep pace with inflation. A year after researchers at Morningstar Inc. recommended a spending cut, the move back to something close to 4% spending rate makes retirement more feasible. This means using Morningstar's updated 3.8% spending recommendation announced in December 2022, someone who retires in December 2022 with $1 million portfolio with 50% in stocks and 50% in bonds would spend no more than $38,000 in 2023. Assuming inflation rises 5% next year, the investor would increase annual spending by that same percentage to $39,900 in 2024 and so on.

31. Fiscal Policy

Fiscal policy refers to the spending and taxing policies of a government and its impact on the citizens of the country. There are two main types of fiscal policy – Expansionary fiscal policy and Contractionary fiscal policy. Expansionary fiscal policy is aimed at boosting the economy by lowering taxes and increasing spending. On the other hand contractionary fiscal policy is designed to reduce economic growth in times of high inflation by increasing taxes and reducing spending.

32. Foreign Direct Investment (FDI)

Foreign direct investment (FDI) refers to the investment in physical assets in one country by an entity in another country.

33. Free Trade Agreement (FTA)

Free trade agreement (FTA) is an agreement between two countries or a group of countries which eliminates trade tariffs and trade barriers and provide protection for investors.

34. Full Employment

Full employment is a situation in which every willing worker in a country is employed and unemployment remains near zero.

35. Gilt-edged Securities (Gilts)

Bonds issued by the UK Government

36. Goldilocks Economy

Goldilocks economy refers to the ideal state of an economy, which has full employment, economic stability, and stable growth. It means that the economy is not expanding or contracting by a large margin.

37. Greenhouse Gases

Greenhouse gases refer to carbon dioxide and other forms of pollution. They trap more sunlight at earth's surface, which gives rise to global warming.

38. Gross Domestic Product (GDP)

Gross Domestic Product (GDP) refers to the monetary value of all goods and services produced within the borders of a country during one year. It is a measure of the health of the economy.

39. Gross National Product (GNP)

GNP is the total value of goods produced and services provided by a country during one year. It is equal to the gross domestic product plus all net income from foreign investments.

40. Hyper-Inflation

A situation of very high inflation resulting from economic and political reasons.

41. Inflation

Inflation is the rate of increase in prices over a given period of time. It is a broad measure of price increase, such as the overall increase in prices or the increase in the cost of living in a country. It is felt as the cost of services and goods that we buy goes up. It means you can buy less goods today for a Rupee compared to what you could buy yesterday. Inflation reduces the value of a currency over time.

42. Imports

Imports refer to the purchase of goods produced in a foreign country by consumers of another country.

43. Industrial Policy

Refers to government policy on industries with a view to ensuring higher industrial production, higher employment and international trade performance.

44. Interest Rates

Interest rate is the rent for money charged by the lender to the borrower. When an individual, entity, or country want to borrow money, the lender would want a compensation for lending money. The compensation is known as interest rate.

45. Keynesian Economics

Keynesian Economics is a macro-economic theory developed by the economist John Maynard Keynes. The theory is based on the idea that government intervention can stabilize an economy.

46. Laissez-Faire

Laissez-Faire is an economic philosophy developed in the 18th century that opposes government intervention in business affairs.

It is also known as 'Free Market', and is based on supply and demand factors.

47. Law of Supply and Demand

The law of supply and demand is based on two economic principles which explains how the changes in the prices of a commodity or product affects its demand and supply. As price increases, supply increases and as a result demand falls. Conversely, as price falls, supply falls and as a result demand goes up.

48. Lipstick Index

Lipstick index is an economic indicator to describe economic trend through the sales of cosmetics. The term was coined by Leonard Lauder, billionaire heir to the Estee Lauder fortune. Estee Lauder is one of the ten largest cosmetics companies in the world. According to Lauder, lipstick sales tend to be inversely correlated to economic health. The speculation is that women substitute lipstick for more expensive purchases like dresses, shoes and perfumes in times of economic distress.

49. Macroeconomics

Macroeconomics is a branch of economics that looks at a country's wider economic picture.

50. Manufacturer's Suggested Retail Price (MSRP)

Manufacturer's Suggested Retail Price (MSRP) is the price at which the manufacturer recommends it to be sold at the point of sale.

51. Maximum Retail Price (MRP)

Maximum Retail Price (MRP) is a manufacturer calculated price that is the highest price at which a product can be sold.

52. Men's Underwear Index (MUI)

The Men's underwear index is an economic index that can point to an economic downturn or the beginning of an economic recovery. This indicator is closely followed by former Federal Reserve Chairman, Alan Greenspan. According to him, in an uncertain economic condition, men will hesitate to buy new undergarments. The premise is that men's underwears are a necessity in normal economic conditions and sales remain stable. During an economic downturn demand for these goods are down as new purchases are postponed. Hence, men's purchasing habit for underwear (and that of their spouses on their behalf) is regarded as a good indicator of consumer spending. In the economic crisis of 2008, this index has proved right. Similarly, indicators from India suggest that undergarment sales have declined towards the end of 2022. We have to wait to see how this impacts the economic performance in coming quarters/years.

53. Microeconomics

Microeconomics is a branch of economics that examines the financial decision making process of individuals, households, and businesses. Microeconomics is the opposite of macroeconomics.

54. Migration

Migration refers to the movement of human beings from one country to another, due to economic, political or various other reasons.

55. Monetarism

Monetarism is a macroeconomic theory which argues that governments can maintain economic stability by targeting the growth rate of money supply.

56. Monetary Policy

Monetary policy refers to the policy of a government and its agencies such as central bank, regarding interest rate levels and other regulations such as banking rules to boost economic growth, manage inflation, and job creation.

57. Nail Polish Index

The "Lipstick index" is a term discussed earlier. Similarly, the sale of nail polish has far outperformed the sale of lipstick in times of economic downturn. It might be because nail polish is cheaper than lipstick. In another way, good nail care is a boon for women. Hence despite economic uncertainty, women concentrate on nail polish more than lipstick.

58. Nominal Exchange Rate

Nominal exchange rate is the price of one currency in terms of another currency. It is expressed as the domestic price of the foreign currency. For example, if it costs 1.1 US dollar for a US person to buy 1 Euro, then from a Euro holder's perspective, €0.91 is one dollar (1/1.1).

59. Phillips Curve

The Phillips curve is an economic theory which states that inflation and unemployment have a stable and inverse relationship. It is developed by William Phillip. It claims that with economic growth comes inflation, which in turn should lead to more jobs and less unemployment.

60. Purchasing Power Parity (PPP)

Purchasing Power Parity (PPP) is an economic theory of comparing the purchasing power of world currencies against one another currency. It is the theoretical exchange rate with which you can buy the same amount of goods with another currency. The Big Mac Index by *The Economist* is a best example of PPP calculation. This index measures the relative under or over valuation of different currencies across countries. The logic behind the Big Mac index is that Big Mac is the same across countries, so it should have the same relative cost from country to country. To explain further, if a Big Mac costs Rs.160 in India and USD 2 in New York, it would imply that 80 Rupees equals to 1 Dollar.

51. Quantitative Easing (QE)

It is one form of economic policy in which the central bank purchases government securities from the market to increase money supply in the economy.

52. Real Exchange Rate (RER)

Real exchange rate between two currencies is the nominal exchange rate multiplied by the ratio of prices between two countries. The core equation is, **RER = eP*/P**, where e is the nominal exchange rate, P* is the average price of a good in the domestic market, and P is the average price of the good in the foreign market. Let's take the example of Big Mac between Germany and USA to explain RER. Let's assume e = 1.10, i.e, 1EUR is 1.10 USD. If the price of a Big Mac in Germany is 2 Euros, and the US price is $2.20, then, (1.1) x (2.00) ÷ (2.20) gives a RER of 1. But, if Big Mac price was 2.20 Euro in Germany, and the US price was $2.20, then the RER would be (1.10) x (2.20) ÷(2.20) = 1.10. This means the Big Mac is costlier by 10% in Germany, compared to the price in U.S.

53. Real Effective Exchange Rate (REER)

The real effective exchange rate (REER) is the weighted average of a country's currency in relation to a basket of other major currencies. A weight based on the trade balance of a country's currency against that of each country in the basket, is used for the calculation.

54. Recommended Retail Price (RRP)

RRP means Recommended Retail Price, which is the suggested retail price by the manufacturers for a product.

55. Senior Citizens

Senior Citizens refer to elderly persons. The definition of senior citizens differ from country to country for various purposes such as banking and taxation. In India a senior citizen is a person who is 60 years or above in age but less than 80 years.

56. Super Senior Citizens

In India a Super Senior Citizen is an individual who is 80 years or above.

57. Sovereign Wealth Fund (SWF)

A sovereign wealth fund (SWF) is a state-owned investment fund that invests in real and financial assets such as stocks, bonds, real estate, precious metals, or in alternative investments such as private equity fund or hedge funds. Sovereign wealth funds invest globally. Sovereign wealth fund is created from the surplus money that a country accrues over time. The fund is also called a Social Wealth Fund.

58. Stagflation

Stagflation is a situation where there is slow economic growth and high unemployment accompanied by high inflation. It is also called a recession-inflation. For example, if there is a sudden surge in the price of a commodity like oil, prices go up and profit comes down.

59. Supply Chain Management (SCM)

Supply chain management (SCM) is the centralized management of the flow of goods and services and includes all processes that transform raw materials into finished goods and services.

60. Wholesale Price Index (WPI)

Wholesale price index (WPI) is a measure of the changes in price at the wholesale level, i.e. price of goods that are exchanged in bulk and traded between wholesale traders. WPI is regarded as an indication of inflation in some economies.

61. Windfall Tax

Windfall Tax is a tax levied by governments on certain industries when such industries generate above average profit due to economic windfall.

Acknowledgements

This book is the result of my career in banking and investments spanning over 45 years. In addition, the curriculum of the CFA programme, which I have undertaken, has made significant contribution to the task of writing this book. The ardent interest I have shown in reading global financial news and investment research from leading global financial companies has instilled in me a keen interest in writing financial books and sharing the knowledge with others. Thus, after writing and publishing two books, "The Bull Run", and "Inside the Foreign Exchange Universe," I took a keen interest in collating the vast amount of banking and investment glossary, I have learnt throughout my career and producing them in the form of a book which I thought many others will benefit and hence this book. Thus, this book is an attempt to share knowledge.

During the process of collecting information for writing this book, I have referred to the public information available on the websites of leading central banks such as Federal Reserve Board, Bank of England, European Central Bank, Bank for International Settlements (BIS) and Reserve Bank of India (RBI). In addition, the information published by several capital market regulators such as U.S Securities and Exchange Commission (SEC), and Securities and Exchange Board of India (SEBI) have helped me a lot in finetuning the glossary definitions included in this book. Further, I am indebted to the text books for my CFA study programme for the knowledge imparted to me. Several banking and investment seminars I attended during my long career have helped expand my knowledge in the capital market sector and enriched me to write this book.

I want to thank my daughter in law Antoinette Gardner who took keen interest in critically evaluating and suggesting corrections to part of this book. I also appreciate the encouragement given to me by all members of my family to make this book a reality.

I am indebted to my publishers Notion Press. for their excellent work in ensuring that this book is printed and published in good time to meet the publishing schedule. Finally, you, the readers are the ultimate beneficiaries of the knowledge shared through this book, and a big thank you to each and every reader.